MW00799249

GoWISE USA Air Fryer Oven Cookbook for Beginners

1000-Day Amazing Recipes for Smart People on a Budget | Fry, Bake, Dehydrate & Roast Most Wanted Family Meals

Nancie Charke

© Copyright 2021 Nancie Charke - All Rights Reserved.

In no way is it legal to reproduce, duplicate, or transmit any part of this document by either electronic means or in printed format. Recording of this publication is strictly prohibited, and any storage of this material is not allowed unless with written permission from the publisher. All rights reserved.

The information provided herein is stated to be truthful and consistent, in that any liability, regarding inattention or otherwise, by any usage or abuse of any policies, processes, or directions contained within is the solitary and complete responsibility of the recipient reader. Under no circumstances will any legal liability or blame be held against the publisher for any reparation, damages, or monetary loss due to the information herein, either directly or indirectly.

Respective authors own all copyrights not held by the publisher.

Legal Notice:

This book is copyright protected. This is only for personal use. You cannot amend, distribute, sell, use, quote or paraphrase any part of the content within this book without the consent of the author or copyright owner. Legal action will be pursued if this is breached.

Disclaimer Notice:

Please note the information contained within this document is for educational and entertainment purposes only. Every attempt has been made to provide accurate, up-to-date and reliable, complete information. No warranties of any kind are expressed or implied. Readers acknowledge that the author is not engaging in the rendering of legal, financial, medical or professional advice.

By reading this document, the reader agrees that under no circumstances are we responsible for any losses, direct or indirect, which are incurred as a result of the use of information contained within this document, including

but not limited to, errors, omissions, or inaccuracies.

Table of Contents

Introduction

Everyone seems to be investing in an air fryer at home nowadays. But what is it about this acclaimed as a miracle gadget that makes people go crazy? Well, imagine your favourite deep-fried food crisped into perfection but sans the oil and all the messy cooking. You bet it suddenly makes your comfort food sound even more comforting.

With a conventional oven, there are two heating plates placed on the top and bottom. The food cooks quicker when you place it near these plates. However, it takes time and does not evenly cook the food. An air fryer is different. They cook the food by heating the air inside the oven. The hot air is then circulated inside by the use of installed fans.

What if you get an air fryer and oven in one cooking appliance? Yes, it is possible. With GoWISE Electric Air Fryer Oven, you won't only get crispy and oil-free food but so much more. Low maintenance and convenience are what make buying an air fryer oven synonymous with getting yourself some extra space, time, and money.

Read on to know how you can take advantage of GoWISE 15-in-1 Electric Air Fryer Oven w/Rotisserie and Dehydrator.

Chapter 1: Breakfast

Breakfast Muffins

Preparation time: 10 minutes
Cooking time: 20 minutes
Servings: 4

Ingredients:

- 1 medium white onion, peeled, chopped
- 4 slices of bacon, chopped
- 2 cups of all-purpose flour
- 1 teaspoon chopped parsley
- ¼ teaspoon salt
- 2 teaspoons baking powder
- ¼ teaspoon ground black pepper
- 3.5 ounces shredded cheddar cheese
- 1 egg
- 2 tablespoons olive oil
- 1 cup milk

Method:

1. Plugin the GoWise Air Fryer Oven, turn it on, insert the wire rack, and then press the menu button to select "manual"; make sure the door of the oven is closed.
2. Press the temp button, and then press the +/- button to adjust the temperature to 350 degrees F, press the time button, and then press the +/- button to adjust the cooking time to 5 minutes and let the air fryer oven preheat.
3. Meanwhile, take a medium skillet pan, place it over medium heat and let it heat until hot.
4. Add chopped bacon, cook for 3 to 4 minutes until almost cooked, add onion and continue cooking for 1 minute, set aside until required.
5. Take a large bowl, place flour in it, add baking powder, salt, black pepper, parsley, and cheese and then stir until mixed.
6. Add the egg
7. pour in milk and oil, whisk until smooth batter comes together, and then stir in bacon-onion mixture until mixed.
8. Take six silicone muffin cups, grease them with oil, and then spoon the prepared batter in them.
9. Arrange the muffin cups on the wire rack, shut the door, press the time button, press the +/- button to adjust the cooking time to 15 minutes, and let it cook until the top turns golden brown.
10. Serve straight away.

Nutrition Value:

- Calories: 110 Cal
- Fat: 8.4 g
- Carbs: 0.1 g
- Protein: 8.6 g

- Fiber: 1.3 g

Cheese and Vegetables Egg Cups

Preparation time: 10 minutes
Cooking time: 12 minutes
Servings: 4

Ingredients:

- 1 cup diced mixed vegetables
- ½ teaspoon salt
- 4 tablespoons half-and-half
- 1 cup shredded cheddar cheese
- ½ teaspoon ground black pepper
- 1 tablespoon chopped cilantro
- 4 eggs

Method:

1. Plugin the GoWise Air Fryer Oven, turn it on, insert the wire rack, and then press the menu button to select "manual"; make sure the door of the oven is closed.
2. Press the temp button, and then press the +/- button to adjust the temperature to 400 degrees F, press the time button, and then press the +/- button to adjust the cooking time to 5 minutes and let the air fryer oven preheat.
3. Meanwhile, take a medium bowl, crack eggs in it and then whisk until combined.
4. Add vegetables, cilantro, salt, black pepper, and half-and-half, whisk until combined, and then divide the mixture into four silicone muffin cups.
5. Arrange the prepared muffin cups on the wire rack, shut the door, press the time button, press the +/- button to adjust the cooking time to 12 minutes, and let it cook until thoroughly cooked.
6. Serve straight away.

Nutrition Value:

- Calories: 105.2 Cal
- Fat: 2.8 g
- Carbs: 4 g
- Protein: 14.6 g
- Fiber: 0.8 g

Five Cheese Pull-Apart Bread

Preparation time: 10 minutes
Cooking time: 10 minutes
Servings: 2

Ingredients:

- 1 medium loaf
- 2 teaspoons minced garlic
- ½ teaspoon salt
- 2 teaspoons chives
- ½ teaspoon ground black pepper
- ½ cup cheddar cheese
- ½ cup grated mozzarella cheese
- 4 ounces crumbled goat cheese
- ½ cup grated Gouda cheese
- 7 tablespoons butter, unsalted
- 4 ounces brie cheese, grated

Method:

1. Take a medium saucepan, place it over medium heat, add butter, and then let it melt.
2. Add garlic, salt, black pepper, and chives, stir until mixed, and then cook for 2 minutes, set aside until required.
3. Plugin the GoWise Air Fryer Oven, turn it on, insert the wire rack, and then press the menu button to select "manual"; make sure the door of the oven is closed.
4. Press the temp button, and then press the +/- button to adjust the temperature to 350 degrees F, press the time button, and then press the +/- button to adjust the cooking time to 5 minutes and let the air fryer oven preheat.
5. Make little slits into the bread with a bread knife, fill each slit with prepared garlic butter until covered, and then insert brie cheese and goat cheese.
6. Cover the top of the bread with Gouda cheese, mozzarella, and cheddar cheese, place it on the wire rack, and then shut the door.
7. Press the time button, press the +/- button to adjust the cooking time to 4 minutes and let it cook until bread is thoroughly warmed and cheese melts completely.
8. Serve straight away.

Nutrition Value:

- Calories: 130 Cal
- Fat: 5 g
- Carbs: 16 g
- Protein: 5 g
- Fiber: 1 g

Bacon and Egg Bites

Preparation time: 10 minutes
Cooking time: 15 minutes
Servings: 6

Ingredients:

- 3 slices of bacon, cooked, crumbled
- ¼ cup chopped white onions
- ¼ cup chopped green bell pepper
- ¼ cup chopped spinach
- ¼ cup chopped red bell pepper
- ½ teaspoon salt
- 6 eggs
- ½ teaspoon ground black pepper
- ½ cup shredded cheddar cheese
- 2 tablespoons heavy whipping cream
- ¼ cup shredded mozzarella cheese

Method:

1. Plugin the GoWise Air Fryer Oven, turn it on, insert the wire rack, and then press the menu button to select "bake"; make sure the door of the oven is closed.
2. Press the temp button, and then press the +/- button to adjust the temperature to 300 degrees F, press the time button, and then press the +/- button to adjust the cooking time to 5 minutes and let the air fryer oven preheat.
3. Meanwhile, take a large bowl, crack the eggs in it, add salt, black pepper, and cream and then whisk until combined.
4. Add half of each bacon, onion, green onion, spinach, green and red bell pepper, and cheese, and then whisk until combined.
5. Take six silicone muffin cups, grease them with oil, evenly pour the egg mixture among them and then sprinkle remaining vegetables and cheese on top.
6. Arrange the muffin cups on the wire rack, shut the door, press the time button, press the +/- button to adjust the cooking time to 15 minutes, and let them cook until firm.
7. Serve straight away.

Nutrition Value:

- Calories: 300 Cal
- Fat: 20 g
- Carbs: 9 g
- Protein: 19 g
- Fiber: 0 g

Spiced Applesauce Bread

Preparation time: 10 minutes
Cooking time: 20 minutes
Servings: 2

Ingredients:

- 2 cups all-purpose flour
- ¼ teaspoon salt
- ¼ teaspoon ground nutmeg
- 1 teaspoon baking soda
- ½ teaspoon ground cinnamon
- ½ teaspoon baking powder
- ¼ teaspoon ground allspice
- 1 ¼ cups applesauce
- 4 egg whites
- 3 tablespoons milk
- 1 cup stevia
- ½ cup olive oil
- ½ cup chopped pecans

Method:

1. Plugin the GoWise Air Fryer Oven, turn it on, insert the wire rack, and then press the menu button to select "bake"; make sure the door of the oven is closed.
2. Press the temp button, press the +/- button to adjust the temperature to 350 degrees F, press the time button, and then press the +/- button to adjust the cooking time to 5 minutes and let the air fryer oven preheat.
3. Meanwhile, take a large bowl, crack the eggs in it, pour in applesauce, oil, and milk, add sugar, and whisk until incorporated.
4. Gradually whisk in flour until incorporated, and then whisk in salt, nutmeg
5. allspice, cinnamon, baking powder, and soda until mixed.
6. Take a 9-inch loaf pan, grease it with oil, spoon the prepared batter in it and then place the pan on the wire rack.
7. Shut the door, press the time button, press the +/- button to adjust the cooking time to 20 minutes, and let it cook until the top turns golden brown.
8. When done, let the bread cool completely, cut it into slices, and then serve.

Nutrition Value:

- Calories: 136.7 Cal
- Fat: 4 g
- Carbs: 23.6 g
- Protein: 2.6 g
- Fiber: 1.5 g

Pumpkin Spice Muffins

Preparation time: 10 minutes
Cooking time: 17 minutes
Servings: 6

Ingredients:

- 1 cup almond flour
- 1 tablespoon stevia
- ½ teaspoon vanilla extract, unsweetened
- ½ teaspoon baking powder
- ½ tablespoon ground cinnamon
- 1 teaspoon pumpkin extract, unsweetened
- 1 tablespoon pumpkin spice seasoning
- 4 tablespoons butter, unsalted, melted
- 2 eggs
- 2 tablespoons chocolate chips, unsweetened

Method:

1. Plugin the GoWise Air Fryer Oven, turn it on, insert the wire rack, and then press the menu button to select "bake"; make sure the door of the oven is closed.
2. Press the temp button, and then press the +/- button to adjust the temperature to 310 degrees F, press the time button, and then press the +/- button to adjust the cooking time to 5 minutes and let the air fryer oven preheat.
3. Meanwhile, take a large bowl, place almond flour in it, add pumpkin spice seasoning
4. cinnamon, sweetener, and baking powder and then stir until mixed.
5. Add pumpkin and vanilla extract, pour in the melted butter, stir until combined, whisk in the egg until blended, and fold in the chocolate chips.
6. Take six silicone muffin cups, and then divide the prepared batter evenly among them.
7. Arrange the prepared muffin cups on the wire rack, shut the door, press the time button, press the +/- button to adjust the cooking time to 17 minutes and let them cook until the batter become firm and the top turn golden brown.
8. Serve straight away.

Nutrition Value:

- Calories: 120 Cal
- Fat: 11 g
- Carbs: 1.7 g
- Protein: 3.3 g
- Fiber: 1 g

Sweet Potato Toast

Preparation time: 10 minutes
Cooking time: 10 minutes
Servings: 4

Ingredients:

- 1 large sweet potato
- 1 teaspoon salt
- 1 teaspoon dried thyme
- 1 teaspoon ground black pepper
- 1 teaspoon dried oregano
- 1 teaspoon dried basil
- 2 tablespoons olive oil

Method:

1. Plugin the GoWise Air Fryer Oven, turn it on, insert the wire rack, and then press the menu button to select "manual"; make sure the door of the oven is closed.
2. Press the temp button, and then press the +/- button to adjust the temperature to 400 degrees F, press the time button, and then press the +/- button to adjust the cooking time to 5 minutes and let the air fryer oven preheat.
3. Meanwhile, prepare the toast and for this, cut off the ends of sweet potato and then cut it into ½-inch thick slices.
4. Brush the sweet potato slices with oil and then season with salt, thyme, black pepper, oregano, and basil.
5. Arrange the prepared sweet potato slices on the wire rack, shut the door, press the time button, press the +/- button to adjust the cooking time to 10 minutes, and let it cook until thoroughly cooked.
6. Serve straight away.

Nutrition Value:

- Calories: 80 Cal
- Fat: 1 g
- Carbs: 18 g
- Protein: 2 g
- Fiber: 3 g

Cranberry Muffins

Preparation time: 10 minutes
Cooking time: 15 minutes
Servings: 6

Ingredients:

- 1 ¾ cup all-purpose flour
- 1 cup cranberries, diced
- 1 teaspoon orange zest
- 3 teaspoons baking powder
- ½ teaspoon salt
- 1 teaspoon lemon zest
- 8 tablespoons sugar
- ¾ cup milk
- 1 egg
- 1/3 cup olive oil

Method:

1. Plugin the GoWise Air Fryer Oven, turn it on, insert the wire rack, and then press the menu button to select "bake"; make sure the door of the oven is closed.
2. Press the temp button, and then press the +/- button to adjust the temperature to 325 degrees F, press the time button, and then press the +/- button to adjust the cooking time to 5 minutes and let the air fryer oven preheat.
3. Meanwhile, take a medium bowl, place cranberries in it, stir in 2 tablespoons sugar until mixed, and then set aside until required.
4. Take a large bowl, place flour in it, add salt, baking powder, and remaining sugar, and then stir until mixed.
5. Pour in oil, milk, and egg
6. whisk until combined, and then fold in orange zest, lemon zest, and cranberries.
7. Take six silicone muffin cups, grease them with oil, and then fill them evenly with the prepared batter.
8. Arrange the muffins on the wire rack, shut the door, press the time button, press the +/- button to adjust the cooking time to 15 minutes, and let it cook until thoroughly cooked.
9. Serve straight away.

Nutrition Value:

- Calories: 214.5 Cal
- Fat: 7 g
- Carbs: 34.5 g
- Protein: 4 g
- Fiber: 1.4 g

Strawberry Rhubarb Crumbles

Preparation time: 10 minutes
Cooking time: 18 minutes
Servings: 4

Ingredients:

- 1 pound strawberries, hulled, halved
- ¾ cup all-purpose flour
- 1 pound rhubarb, trimmed, cut into ½ inch pieces
- 1 tablespoon cornstarch
- ¼ teaspoon salt
- ¼ cup and 3 tablespoons sugar, divided
- ¼ cup unsalted almonds, chopped
- 6 tablespoons unsalted butter, chopped

Method:

1. Plugin the GoWise Air Fryer Oven, turn it on, insert the wire rack, and then press the menu button to select "manual"; make sure the door of the oven is closed.
2. Press the temp button, and then press the +/- button to adjust the temperature to 350 degrees F, press the time button, and then press the +/- button to adjust the cooking time to 5 minutes and let the air fryer oven preheat.
3. Meanwhile, take a large bowl, place berries and rhubarb in it, add cornstarch and ¼ cup sugar and then stir until mixed.
4. Take a separate large bowl, place flour in it, add butter and then rub it with fingers until the mixture resembles crumbs.
5. Add salt, almonds, and remaining sugar, and then stir until well combined.
6. Take four 8-ounce ramekins, grease them with butter, fill them with fruit mixture, and cover the top with flour mixture.
7. Arrange the ramekins on the wire rack, shut the door, press the time button, press the +/- button to adjust the cooking time to 18 minutes, and let it cook until thoroughly cooked and the top turn golden brown.
8. Serve straight away.

Nutrition Value:

- Calories: 317.4 Cal
- Fat: 8 g
- Carbs: 57.7 g
- Protein: 6 g
- Fiber: 6.1 g

French Toast Sticks

Preparation time: 10 minutes
Cooking time: 10 minutes
Servings: 2

Ingredients:

- 4 slices of bread
- ½ teaspoon ground cinnamon
- 1 teaspoon vanilla extract, unsweetened
- 2/3 cup milk
- 3 eggs
- ½ tablespoon powdered sugar

Method:

1. Plugin the GoWise Air Fryer Oven, turn it on, insert the wire rack and drip pan and then press the menu button to select "manual"; make sure the door of the oven is closed.
2. Press the temp button, and then press the +/- button to adjust the temperature to 370 degrees F, press the time button, and then press the +/- button to adjust the cooking time to 5 minutes and let the air fryer oven preheat.
3. Meanwhile, take a shallow dish, crack the eggs in it, whisk until blended and then whisk in cinnamon, vanilla, and milk until combined.
4. Cut the bread slices vertically into sticks, and then dip each into the egg mixture.
5. Arrange the breadsticks on the wire rack, shut the door, press the time button, press the +/- button to adjust the cooking time to 10 minutes, and let it cook until golden brown, flipping halfway.
6. When done, sprinkle powdered sugar over the toast sticks and then serve.

Nutrition Value:

- Calories: 222.4 Cal
- Fat: 11.6 g
- Carbs: 27 g
- Protein: 4 g
- Fiber: 1 g

Jalapeno Cornbread

Preparation time: 10 minutes
Cooking time: 20 minutes
Servings: 4

Ingredients:

- ½ cup chopped jalapenos
- 1 cup yellow cornmeal
- 2 teaspoons baking powder
- 1 cup all-purpose flour
- 1 teaspoon salt
- ½ cup of sugar
- ½ teaspoon baking soda
- 3 tablespoons butter, unsalted, melted
- 2 tablespoons olive oil
- ½ cup buttermilk
- ¼ cup grated pepper jack cheese
- ¾ cup sour cream
- 2 eggs

Method:

1. Plugin the GoWise Air Fryer Oven, turn it on, insert the wire rack, and then press the menu button to select "manual"; make sure the door of the oven is closed.
2. Press the temp button, and then press the +/- button to adjust the temperature to 300 degrees F, press the time button, and then press the +/- button to adjust the cooking time to 5 minutes and let the air fryer oven preheat.
3. Meanwhile, take a large bowl, place flour in it, add cornmeal, salt, sugar, baking soda, and powder and then stir until mixed.
4. Take a separate medium bowl, crack the eggs in it, add butter, pour in sour cream, oil, and milk, and then whisk until combined.
5. Pour egg mixture into the flour mixture, whisk until incorporated and smooth batter comes together, and then fold in cheese and jalapeno until mixed.
6. Take a loaf pan, grease it with oil, spoon the batter in it, place it on the wire rack, and then shut the door.
7. Press the time button, press the +/- button to adjust the cooking time to 20 minutes and let it cook until the top turn golden brown, turning the pan halfway.
8. When done, let the bread cool slightly, cut it into slices, and then serve.

Nutrition Value:

- Calories: 160 Cal
- Fat: 6 g
- Carbs: 25 g
- Protein: 3 g
- Fiber: 0.5 g

Bread Rolls

Preparation time: 1 hour and 15 minutes
Cooking time: 15 minutes
Servings: 4

Ingredients:

- 3 cups all-purpose flour
- 1 teaspoon salt
- 1 teaspoon active yeast
- 1 teaspoon ground black pepper
- 8 tablespoons butter, unsalted
- 1 tablespoon olive oil
- 1 tablespoon coconut oil
- 1 cup milk

Method:

1. Take a large bowl, place flour in it, and then stir in butter until mixed.
2. Take a medium saucepan, place it over medium heat, pour in milk, stir in coconut oil and olive oil and then cook for 3 to 4 minutes until lukewarm.
3. Pour the milk into the flour bowl, add yeast, and stir until combined.
4. Transfer the mixture onto a cleaned working space dusted with flour, knead for 5 minutes until a smooth dough comes together, cover the dough with a damp cloth and let it rest for 30 minutes at a warm place.
5. After 30 minutes, knead the dough for another 5 minutes, cover it again with a damp cloth and then let it rest for another 30 minutes.
6. Then divide the dough into the evenly sized portion, and shape each portion into a ball.
7. Plugin the GoWise Air Fryer Oven, turn it on, insert a parchment-lined wire rack, and then press the menu button to select "manual"; make sure the door of the oven is closed.
8. Press the temp button, and then press the +/- button to adjust the temperature to 350 degrees F, press the time button, and then press the +/- button to adjust the cooking time to 5 minutes and let the air fryer oven preheat.
9. Then arrange the prepared balls on the wire rack, shut the door, press the time button, press the +/- button to adjust the cooking time to 15 minutes, and let it cook until nicely golden brown.
10. Serve straight away.

Nutrition Value:

- Calories: 180 Cal
- Fat: 1 g
- Carbs: 33 g
- Protein: 5 g
- Fiber: 1 g

Egg in a Hole

Preparation time: 5 minutes
Cooking time: 6 minutes
Servings: 2

Ingredients:

- 1 slice of bread
- 1 egg
- 1/8 teaspoon salt
- 1/8 teaspoon ground black pepper

Method:

1. Plugin the GoWise Air Fryer Oven, turn it on, insert the wire rack, and then press the menu button to select "manual"; make sure the door of the oven is closed.
2. Press the temp button, and then press the +/- button to adjust the temperature to 330 degrees F, press the time button, and then press the +/- button to adjust the cooking time to 5 minutes and let the air fryer oven preheat.
3. Meanwhile, take a heatproof baking pan and then grease it with oil.
4. Make a hole in the center of the bread slice with a round cookie cutter, place the bread slice into the prepared pan and then crack the egg in it.
5. Place the baking pan on the wire rack, shut the door, press the time button, press the +/- button to adjust the cooking time to 6 minutes, and let it cook until the egg has cooked to the desired level.
6. Sprinkle salt and black pepper over the egg and then serve.

Nutrition Value:

- Calories: 181.2 Cal
- Fat: 10.1 g
- Carbs: 13.8 g
- Protein: 9.1 g
- Fiber: 1.8 g

Apple, Pecan and Quinoa Granola

Preparation time: 10 minutes
Cooking time: 5 hours and 10 minutes
Servings: 4

Ingredients:

- 1 medium apple, cored, sliced
- 1 cup rolled oats
- 1 cup chopped pecans
- 1/3 cup quinoa, uncooked
- 2 tablespoons ground flaxseed
- 1 teaspoon ground cinnamon
- 1/8 teaspoon salt
- ¼ teaspoon ground nutmeg
- ¼ cup maple syrup
- 3 tablespoons melted coconut oil
- ½ cup applesauce, unsweetened

Method:

1. Plugin the GoWise Air Fryer Oven, turn it on, insert the wire rack, and then press the menu button to select "manual"; make sure the door of the oven is closed.
2. Then arrange the apple slices on the wire rack, return them into the air fryer oven, and shut the door.
3. Press the menu button to select "dehydrate," press the time button, and then press the +/- button to adjust the cooking time to 5 hours and let the apple slices dehydrate.
4. Take a medium bowl, place oats in it, add pecans, flaxseeds, and quinoa, and then stir in salt, cinnamon, and nutmeg
5. Take a separate medium bowl, pour applesauce in it, add maple syrup and coconut oil, and then stir until combined.
6. When apple slices have dehydrated, pour the applesauce mixture into the oats mixture, add apple slices and then stir until combined.
7. Spread the granola mixture evenly onto the mesh racks in a single layer, arrange the racks into the air fryer oven, press the menu button to select "bake," press the time button, and then press the +/- button to adjust the cooking time to 10 minutes.
8. When done, let the granola cool completely and then serve.

Nutrition Value:

- Calories: 157.1 Cal
- Fat: 6 g
- Carbs: 22.3 g
- Protein: 4.5 g
- Fiber: 3 g

Avocado Egg Boat

Preparation time: 10 minutes
Cooking time: 8 minutes
Servings: 4

Ingredients:

- 2 large avocado, pitted
- 2 teaspoons chopped parsley
- 1 teaspoon salt
- 2 teaspoons chopped chives
- 1 teaspoon ground black pepper
- 4 eggs

Method:

1. Plugin the GoWise Air Fryer Oven, turn it on, insert the wire rack, and then press the menu button to select "manual"; make sure the door of the oven is closed.
2. Press the temp button, press the +/- button to adjust the temperature to 350 degrees F, press the time button, and then press the +/- button to adjust the cooking time to 5 minutes and let the air fryer oven preheat.
3. Meanwhile, prepare the avocados, remove their pit, season them with salt, black pepper, chives, and parsley and then crack the eggs in avocado halves.
4. Arrange the prepared avocado egg boats on the wire rack, shut the door, press the time button, press the +/- button to adjust the cooking time to 8 minutes, and let it cook.
5. Serve straight away.

Nutrition Value:

- Calories: 224 Cal
- Fat: 19 g
- Carbs: 9 g
- Protein: 7.5 g
- Fiber: 6.5 g

Chapter 2: Poultry

Korean BBQ Chicken Skewers

Preparation time: 2 hours and 10 minutes
Cooking time: 10 minutes
Servings: 8

Ingredients:

- 1 medium red bell pepper, cored, cut into large chunks
- 2 pounds chicken breasts, cubed

- 2 scallions, chopped
- 1 tablespoon sesame seeds

Korean BBQ Marinade:

- 1 ½ teaspoon minced garlic
- ¼ cup grated red onion
- 1 tablespoon grated ginger
- ¾ cup brown sugar

- 2 tablespoons chili-garlic sauce
- 1 cup of soy sauce
- 1 tablespoon sesame oil
- 2 tablespoons of rice wine vinegar

Korean BBQ Sauce:

- 1 tablespoon cornstarch
- 1 cup Korean BBQ Marinade

- 1 tablespoon cold water

Method:

1. Prepare the marinade and for this, take a medium bowl, place all of its ingredients in it, and then stir until well mixed.
2. Reserve 1 cup of the prepared marinade, pour the remaining marinade in a large bowl, add chicken pieces, toss until coated, and then let it refrigerator for a minimum of 2 hours.
3. Meanwhile, prepare the BBQ sauce and for this, take a small saucepan, place it over medium heat, add reserved 1 cup of marinade and then bring it to a boil.
4. Then switch heat to medium-low level, and simmer the marinade for 5 minutes.
5. Stir together cornstarch and water, add to the simmering marinade and then continue cooking for 4 minutes until thickened; set aside until required.
6. Plugin the GoWise Air Fryer Oven, turn it on, insert the drip pan, and then press the menu button to select "chicken"; make sure the door of the oven is closed.
7. Press the temp button, and then press the +/- button to adjust the temperature to 350 degrees F, press the time button, and then press the +/- button to adjust the cooking time to 5 minutes and let the air fryer oven preheat.

8. Meanwhile, take the GoWise Rotisserie Skewers and then thread chicken and red bell pepper pieces in alternate positions.
9. Insert the Rotisserie Skewers into the heated air fryer oven, shut the door, press the time button, press the +/- button to adjust the cooking time to 5 minutes and let it cook.
10. Brush the prepared BBQ sauce over the chicken and red bell pepper, and then continue cooking for 5 minutes until the chicken has thoroughly cooked.
11. When done, sprinkle sesame seeds and scallions over the skewers and then serve.

Nutrition Value:

- Calories: 171 Cal
- Fat: 10 g
- Carbs: 12 g
- Protein: 8 g
- Fiber: 1 g

Chicken Bombers

Preparation time: 10 minutes
Cooking time: 13 minutes
Servings: 2

Ingredients:

- 2 pounds chicken breast, skinless
- 12 slices of bacon
- 1 tablespoon chopped chives
- 8 ounces cream cheese, softened

Method:

1. Plugin the GoWise Air Fryer Oven, turn it on, insert the drip pan with mesh basket and then press the menu button to select "chicken"; make sure the door of the oven is closed.
2. Press the temp button, and then press the +/- button to adjust the temperature to 450 degrees F, press the time button, and then press the +/- button to adjust the cooking time to 5 minutes and let the air fryer oven preheat.
3. Meanwhile, pound the chicken breast with a meat mallet and then cut each chicken breast into six strips.
4. Spread cream cheese on a chicken strip, roll it up, wrap with a bacon slice and then repeat with the remaining chicken strips.
5. Arrange the chicken rolls on the mesh basket, shut the door, press the time button, press the +/- button to adjust the cooking time to 13 minutes, and let it cook.
6. Serve straight away.

Nutrition Value:

- Calories: 399 Cal
- Fat: 36 g
- Carbs: 2 g
- Protein: 16 g
- Fiber: 1 g

Orange Chicken

Preparation time: 10 minutes
Cooking time: 10 minutes
Servings: 4

Ingredients:

- 2 tablespoons cornstarch
- 1 pound chicken breasts, skinless

For The Orange Sauce:

- 1 orange, zested
- ¼ teaspoon ground ginger
- 2 tablespoons brown sugar
- 1/8 teaspoon red pepper flakes
- 2 teaspoons cornstarch
- 1 tablespoon soy sauce
- 1 tablespoon rice wine vinegar
- 2 tablespoons water
- ½ cup of orange juice

Method:

1. Plugin the GoWise Air Fryer Oven, turn it on, insert the drip pan with mesh racks and then press the menu button to select "chicken"; make sure the door of the oven is closed.
2. Press the temp button, and then press the +/- button to adjust the temperature to 400 degrees F, press the time button, and then press the +/- button to adjust the cooking time to 5 minutes and let the air fryer oven preheat.
3. Meanwhile, cut the chicken into cubes, place them into a large bowl, add cornstarch and then toss until coated.
4. Arrange the coated chicken pieces on the mesh racks, shut the door, press the time button, press the +/- button to adjust the cooking time to 10 minutes, and let it cook.
5. Meanwhile, prepare the sauce, and for this, take a small saucepan, place it over medium heat and then add all the ingredients in it except for water and cornstarch.
6. Whisk until combined, simmer the sauce for 5 minutes and then whisk in cornstarch and water until combined.
7. Continue simmering the sauce for 2 minutes until thickened and then remove the pan from heat, set aside until required.
8. When chicken has cooked, drizzle the sauce over the chicken pieces, toss until coated, and then serve.

Nutrition Value:

- Calories: 315 Cal
- Fat: 7.5 g
- Carbs: 23 g

- Protein: 37.5 g
- Fiber: 23 g

Italian Chicken Skewers

Preparation time: 40 minutes
Cooking time: 10 minutes
Servings: 4

Ingredients:

- 1 French baguette, cut into cubes
- 1 pound chicken breasts, skinless, cubed
- 1 ½ teaspoon minced garlic
- 1 teaspoon salt
- ½ teaspoon ground black pepper
- 2 tablespoons tomato paste
- 1 tablespoon chopped parsley
- ¼ cup olive oil, plus more for drizzling

Method:

1. Take a medium bowl, place chicken pieces in it, add salt and black pepper and then toss until coated.
2. Take a separate medium bowl, add garlic, parsley, oil, and tomato paste, whisk until combined, and then transfer this mixture into a large plastic bag
3. Add chicken pieces into the plastic bag
4. seal it, turn it upside down until coated, and then let it marinate for 30 minutes in the refrigerator.
5. Then Plugin the GoWise Air Fryer Oven, turn it on, and then press the menu button to select "chicken"; make sure the door of the oven is closed.
6. Press the temp button, and then press the +/- button to adjust the temperature to 400 degrees F, press the time button, and then press the +/- button to adjust the cooking time to 5 minutes and let the air fryer oven preheat.
7. Meanwhile, take the GoWise Rotisserie Skewers and then thread chicken and bread cubes in alternate positions.
8. Insert the Rotisserie Skewers into the heated air fryer oven, shut the door, press the time button, press the +/- button to adjust the cooking time to 10 minutes, and let it cook.
9. Serve straight away.

Nutrition Value:

- Calories: 350.2 Cal
- Fat: 7.6 g
- Carbs: 11.3 g
- Protein: 56 g
- Fiber: 2.6 g

Cherry Glazed Chicken Wings

Preparation time: 10 minutes
Cooking time: 25 minutes
Servings: 4

Ingredients:

- 12 chicken wings
- 3 teaspoons salt, divided
- ½ tablespoon minced garlic
- 1 teaspoon ground black pepper, divided
- 1 tablespoon Worcestershire sauce
- ½ cup apple cider vinegar
- 1 cup ketchup
- ½ cup cherry preserves
- 3 tablespoons olive oil, divided
- 2 tablespoons hot sauce

Method:

1. Take a small saucepan, place it over medium heat, add 1 tablespoon oil and then let it heat until hot.
2. Stir in garlic, cook for 1 minute until fragrant, and then add 1 teaspoon salt, ½ teaspoon ground black pepper, cherry preserve, ketchup, vinegar, hot sauce, and Worcestershire sauce.
3. Whisk until combined and then cook for 2 minutes until thoroughly hot, set aside until required.
4. Plugin the GoWise Air Fryer Oven, turn it on, insert the drip pan with mesh racks and then press the menu button to select "wings"; make sure the door of the oven is closed.
5. Press the temp button, press the +/- button to adjust the temperature to 350 degrees F, press the time button, and then press the +/- button to adjust the cooking time to 5 minutes and let the air fryer oven preheat.
6. Meanwhile, brush the chicken wings with the remaining oil, season with the remaining salt and black pepper, and then arrange the chicken wings on the mesh racks.
7. Shut the door of the air fryer oven, press the time button, press the +/- button to adjust the cooking time to 15 minutes, and let it cook, flipping halfway.
8. Brush the chicken wings with prepared sauce and then continue cooking for 5 minutes until glazed.
9. Serve straight away.

Nutrition Value:

- Calories: 214 Cal
- Fat: 12 g
- Carbs: 15 g
- Protein: 12 g
- Fiber: 2 g

Hot Wings

Preparation time: 10 minutes
Cooking time: 15 minutes
Servings: 2

Ingredients:

- 10 chicken wings
- ½ cup all-purpose flour
- 1/8 teaspoon garlic powder
- ¼ teaspoon salt
- ¼ teaspoon paprika
- 1/8 teaspoon ground black pepper
- ¼ teaspoon cayenne pepper
- ¼ cup hot sauce
- ½ stick of butter, unsalted
- 2 tablespoons olive oil

Method:

1. Plugin the GoWise Air Fryer Oven, turn it on, insert the drip pan and mesh racks and then press the menu button to select "wings"; make sure the door of the oven is closed.
2. Press the temp button, and then press the +/- button to adjust the temperature to 370 degrees F, press the time button, and then press the +/- button to adjust the cooking time to 5 minutes and let the air fryer oven preheat.
3. Meanwhile, take a small bowl, place flour in it, add garlic powder, salt, paprika, black pepper, and cayenne pepper and then stir until mixed.
4. Working on one chicken wing at a time, dredge it into the flour mixture and then drizzle with oil.
5. Arrange the chicken wings on the mesh racks, shut the door of the air fryer oven, press the time button, press the +/- button to adjust the cooking time to 15 minutes, and let it cook, turning halfway.
6. Meanwhile, prepare the sauce and for this, take a small saucepan, place it over medium heat, and then add butter and hot sauce.
7. Cook for 4 to 5 minutes until butter melts, stirring continuously, and then remove the pan from heat, set aside until required.
8. When the chicken wings have cooked, drizzle the cooked sauce over them and then toss until thoroughly coated.
9. Serve straight away.

Nutrition Value:

- Calories: 172 Cal
- Fat: 10.4 g
- Carbs: 11 g
- Protein: 12.6 g
- Fiber: 1 g

Herb Rubbed Chicken Thighs

Preparation time: 40 minutes
Cooking time: 15 minutes
Servings: 2

Ingredients:

- 1 pound chicken thighs, skinless
- 1 teaspoon dried rosemary
- 1 tablespoon minced garlic
- 1 teaspoon salt
- ½ teaspoon lemon pepper
- 1 teaspoon dried thyme
- ½ teaspoon ground black pepper
- 1 lemon, juiced

Method:

1. Prepare the chicken and for this, season the chicken thighs with salt and black pepper.
2. Place the chicken thighs into a large bowl, add remaining ingredients, toss until well coated, and then let them marinate for 30 minutes in the refrigerator.
3. Then Plugin the GoWise Air Fryer Oven, turn it on, insert the drip pan with mesh racks and then press the menu button to select "chicken"; make sure the door of the oven is closed.
4. Press the temp button, and then press the +/- button to adjust the temperature to 360 degrees F, press the time button, and then press the +/- button to adjust the cooking time to 5 minutes and let the air fryer oven preheat.
5. Arrange marinated chicken thighs on the mesh racks, shut the door of the air fryer oven, press the time button, press the +/- button to adjust the cooking time to 15 minutes, and let it cook, flipping halfway.
6. Serve straight away.

Nutrition Value:

- Calories: 327 Cal
- Fat: 18.2 g
- Carbs: 22 g
- Protein: 18.2 g
- Fiber: 1.8 g

Rotisserie Chicken

Preparation time: 10 minutes
Cooking time: 60 minutes
Servings: 2

Ingredients:

- 3 pounds of Rotisserie chicken, cleaned
- 2 tablespoons coconut oil
- 1 tablespoon all-purpose seasoning

Method:

1. Plugin the GoWise Air Fryer Oven, turn it on, insert the drip pan and then press the menu button to select "chicken"; make sure the door of the oven is closed.
2. Press the temp button, and then press the +/- button to adjust the temperature to 350 degrees F, press the time button, and then press the +/- button to adjust the cooking time to 5 minutes and let the air fryer oven preheat.
3. Meanwhile, brush the chicken with coconut oil, season with all-purpose seasoning until coated, and then arrange it into the Rotisserie fork.
4. Place the chicken Rotisserie form into the air fryer oven, shut the door, press the time button, press the +/- button to adjust the cooking time to 30 minutes, and let it cook.
5. Then turn the chicken, and continue cooking it for 30 minutes until thoroughly cooked and chicken turns tender.
6. When done, carve the chicken into pieces and then serve.

Nutrition Value:

- Calories: 475 Cal
- Fat: 36 g
- Carbs: 0 g
- Protein: 35 g
- Fiber: 0 g

Breaded Whole Chicken

Preparation time: 10 minutes
Cooking time: 50 minutes
Servings: 4

Ingredients:

- 3 pounds whole chicken, cleaned, rinsed
- 2/3 cup Bisquick mix
- 1 ¼ teaspoon salt
- 1 ½ teaspoon paprika
- ¼ teaspoon ground black pepper
- 1 tablespoon butter, unsalted, melted

Method:

1. Plugin the GoWise Air Fryer Oven, turn it on, insert the drip pan, and then press the menu button to select "chicken"; make sure the door of the oven is closed.
2. Press the temp button, and then press the +/- button to adjust the temperature to 425 degrees F, press the time button, and then press the +/- button to adjust the cooking time to 5 minutes and let the air fryer oven preheat.
3. Meanwhile, take a medium bowl, place Bisquick mix in it, add salt, black pepper, and paprika and then stir until combined.
4. Brush the butter on all sides of the chicken, coat the chicken with the Bisquick mixture, arrange it into the Rotisserie fork.
5. Place the chicken Rotisserie form into the air fryer oven, shut the door, press the time button, press the +/- button to adjust the cooking time to 35 minutes, and let it cook.
6. Then turn the chicken, and continue cooking it for 15 minutes until thoroughly cooked and chicken turns tender.
7. When done, carve the chicken into pieces and then serve.

Nutrition Value:

- Calories: 348 Cal
- Fat: 7.5 g
- Carbs: 1 g
- Protein: 69 g
- Fiber: 0.6 g

Orange Soda Chicken Wings

Preparation time: 10 minutes
Cooking time: 25 minutes
Servings: 4

Ingredients:

- 2 pounds chicken wings, cut in half at joint
- ½ teaspoon garlic powder
- ½ teaspoon salt
- ½ teaspoon onion powder
- ¼ teaspoon ground black pepper
- 1 tablespoon baking powder

For the Sauce:

- 1 tablespoon orange zest
- ¼ teaspoon crushed red pepper flakes
- 1 tablespoons cornstarch
- 2 tablespoons brown sugar
- 1 teaspoon soy sauce
- 2 tablespoons butter
- 3 tablespoons hot sauce
- 1 cup orange soda

Method:

1. Plugin the GoWise Air Fryer Oven, turn it on, insert the drip pan and mesh racks and then press the menu button to select "wings"; make sure the door of the oven is closed.
2. Press the temp button, and then press the +/- button to adjust the temperature to 360 degrees F, press the time button, and then press the +/- button to adjust the cooking time to 5 minutes and let the air fryer oven preheat.
3. Meanwhile, take a large bowl, place chicken wings in it, season with salt, black pepper, onion powder, baking powder, and garlic powder, and then toss until coated.
4. Arrange the chicken wings on the mesh racks, shut the door, press the time button, press the +/- button to adjust the cooking time to 25 minutes, and let it cook.
5. Meanwhile, prepare the sauce and for this, take a medium saucepan, place it over medium heat, and then add all of its ingredients.
6. Stir until well combined, and then cook the sauce for 20 minutes until the sauce has thickened, set aside until required.
7. When chicken wings have cooked, add them to the sauce and then toss until coated.
8. Serve straight away.

Nutrition Value:

- Calories: 260 Cal
- Fat: 13 g
- Carbs: 23 g

- Protein: 12 g
- Fiber: 2 g

Greek Chicken Kebabs

Preparation time: 55 minutes
Cooking time: 20 minutes
Servings: 6

Ingredients:

- 2 large red bell peppers, cored, 1 ¼ inch diced
- 1 large red onion, peeled, 1 ¼ inch diced
- 1 ¾ pounds chicken breasts, skinless, 1 ¼ inch cubed
- 3 small zucchinis, ½ inch sliced
- 1 ½ teaspoon minced garlic
- ½ teaspoon ground coriander
- 2 teaspoons dried oregano
- ¾ teaspoon salt
- ½ teaspoon dried basil
- ½ teaspoon ground black pepper
- ½ teaspoon dried thyme
- 1 tablespoon red wine vinegar
- 3 tablespoons lemon juice
- ¼ cup and 2 tablespoons olive oil, divided

Method:

1. Take a medium bowl, pour in ¼ cup oil, add salt, black pepper, coriander, basil, thyme, oregano, garlic, lemon juice, and vinegar and then whisk until combined.
2. Take a large plastic bag
3. pour in the oil mixture, add chicken pieces, and then seal the bag
4. Turn the plastic bag upside down until coated, place it into the refrigerator, and then let the chicken marinate for 45 minutes.
5. Meanwhile, take a large bowl, place all the vegetable pieces, drizzle with remaining oil, season with ½ teaspoon salt and then toss until coated.
6. Then Plugin the GoWise Air Fryer Oven, turn it on, and then press the menu button to select "chicken"; make sure the door of the oven is closed.
7. Press the temp button, press the +/- button to adjust the temperature to 400 degrees F, press the time button, and then press the +/- button to adjust the cooking time to 5 minutes and let the air fryer oven preheat.
8. Meanwhile, take the GoWise Rotisserie Skewers and then thread two pieces of marinated chicken and a piece of zucchini, onion, and bell pepper.
9. Insert the Rotisserie Skewers into the heated air fryer oven, shut the door, press the time button, press the +/- button to adjust the cooking time to 10 minutes, and let it cook.
10. When done, transfer cooked chicken and vegetables to a plate, keep warm and then repeat with the remaining chicken and vegetable pieces.

11. Serve straight away.

Nutrition Value:

- Calories: 206 Cal
- Fat: 5.1 g
- Carbs: 1.1 g

- Protein: 36.5 g
- Fiber: 0.1 g

Chapter 3: Beef

Mexican Beef Kebabs

Preparation time: 10 minutes
Cooking time: 15 minutes
Servings: 2

Ingredients:

- 1 ½ pound rib-eye steak, cut into 1-inch cubes
- 1 medium red bell pepper, cored, 1-inch cubed
- 1 medium green pepper, cored, 1-inch cubed
- 3 thick slices of bacon, cut into 1-inch pieces
- ½ of a medium white onion, peeled, 1-inch cubed
- 1 teaspoon salt
- 1 teaspoon ground black pepper
- 1 ½ tablespoon olive oil

Method:

1. Plugin the GoWise Air Fryer Oven, turn it on, insert the drip pan, and then press the menu button to select "steak"; make sure the door of the oven is closed.
2. Press the temp button, and then press the +/- button to adjust the temperature to 400 degrees F, press the time button, and then press the +/- button to adjust the cooking time to 5 minutes and let the air fryer oven preheat.
3. Meanwhile, take a large bowl, place steak pieces in it, add salt and black pepper, drizzle with oil and then toss until coated.
4. Thread the steak pieces and vegetable pieces on the Rotisserie Skewers and then arrange them in the air fryer oven.
5. Shut the door of the air fryer oven, press the time button, press the +/- button to adjust the cooking time to 15 minutes, and let it cook.
6. Serve straight away.

Nutrition Value:

- Calories: 290 Cal
- Fat: 19.6 g
- Carbs: 5.4 g
- Protein: 22.3 g
- Fiber: 1.6 g

Marinated Steaks

Preparation time: 10 minutes
Cooking time: 15 minutes
Servings: 6

Ingredients:

- 6 rib-eye steak, boneless
- 1 tablespoon salt
- ½ cup chopped chives
- 2 tablespoons onion powder
- 1 tablespoon ground cumin
- 2 tablespoons garlic powder
- 2 tablespoons paprika
- 1 tablespoon ground black pepper
- 2 tablespoons dried oregano
- 1 cup soy sauce

Method:

1. Take a small bowl, place all the seasonings and spices in it and then stir until mixed.
2. Dredge the steaks into the prepared spice mixture and then place them in a large plastic bag
3. Pour soy sauce into the plastic bag
4. seal it and then let the steak marinate for 1 hour in the refrigerator.
5. Then Plugin the GoWise Air Fryer Oven, turn it on, insert the drip pan, and then press the menu button to select "steak"; make sure the door of the oven is closed.
6. Press the temp button, and then press the +/- button to adjust the temperature to 400 degrees F, press the time button, and then press the +/- button to adjust the cooking time to 5 minutes and let the air fryer oven preheat.
7. Place the marinated steaks in the Rotisserie Steak Cage, arrange it into the air fryer oven, shut the door, press the time button, press the +/- button to adjust the cooking time to 15 minutes, and let it cook until cooked to the desired level.
8. When done, let the steaks rest for 5 minutes, sprinkle with chives and then serve.

Nutrition Value:

- Calories: 274.5 Cal
- Fat: 9.7 g
- Carbs: 8.3 g
- Protein: 35.6 g
- Fiber: 0.6 g

Vegetables, Corn and Beef Kabobs

Preparation time: 1 hour and 10 minutes
Cooking time: 12 minutes
Servings: 8

Ingredients:

- 1 ½ pound beef should steak, cut into cubes
- 1 large green bell pepper, cored, diced
- 1 medium yellow squash, diced

- 1 large red bell pepper, cored, diced
- 1 teaspoon salt
- 1 teaspoon ground black pepper
- 2 corn on Kob, cut into segments

For the Marinade:

- 1 teaspoon cayenne pepper
- 1 teaspoon paprika
- 1 teaspoon red pepper flakes

- 1/3 cup soy sauce
- ¼ cup steak sauce
- 2 tablespoons white vinegar

Method:

1. Take a small bowl, place all the ingredients for the marinade in it and then whisk until combined.
2. Pour the marinade in a large plastic bag
3. add steak pieces in it, seal the bag
4. turn it upside down until coated, and then let it marinate for 1 hour in the refrigerator.
5. Plugin the GoWise Air Fryer Oven, turn it on, insert the drip pan with a wire rack, and then press the menu button to select "steak"; make sure the door of the oven is closed.
6. Press the temp button, and then press the +/- button to adjust the temperature to 370 degrees F, press the time button, and then press the +/- button to adjust the cooking time to 5 minutes and let the air fryer oven preheat.
7. Meanwhile, thread marinated steak pieces, vegetables, and corn pieces into Rotisserie Skewers, arrange them into the air fryer oven, and then shut the door.
8. Press the time button, press the +/- button to adjust the cooking time to 12 minutes and let it cook.
9. Serve straight away.

Nutrition Value:

- Calories: 247.6 Cal
- Fat: 11 g
- Carbs: 3.4 g

- Protein: 31.2 g
- Fiber: 1 g

Egg Rolls

Preparation time: 15 minutes
Cooking time: 15 minutes
Servings: 12

Ingredients:

- ½ cup leftover corned beef
- ¼ cup grated carrot
- ¼ cup grated cabbage
- ¼ cup grated potato
- ¼ cup grated Swiss cheese
- 12 egg roll wrappers
- ½ cup of water

Method:

1. Take a large bowl, place beef in it, add carrot, cabbage, potatoes, and cheese and then stir until well combined.
2. Prepare the rolls and for this, place an egg roll wrapper in a clean working space, place 2 tablespoons of beef mixture in it, brush water on the edges of the wrapper and then roll it.
3. Then Plugin the GoWise Air Fryer Oven, turn it on, insert the wire rack, and then press the menu button to select "manual"; make sure the door of the oven is closed.
4. Press the temp button, press the +/- button to adjust the temperature to 400 degrees F, press the time button, and then press the +/- button to adjust the cooking time to 5 minutes and let the air fryer oven preheat.
5. Arrange the prepared egg rolls on the wire rack, shut the door, press the time button, press the +/- button to adjust the cooking time to 15 minutes, and let it cook until nicely golden brown, turning halfway.
6. Serve straight away.

Nutrition Value:

- Calories: 112.6 Cal
- Fat: 0.6 g
- Carbs: 22.5 g
- Protein: 4.3 g
- Fiber: 1.5 g

Steak

Preparation time: 10 minutes
Cooking time: 15 minutes
Servings: 1

Ingredients:

- 1 bone-in ribeye steak, about 2 pounds
- 1 teaspoon minced garlic
- 1 teaspoon salt
- 1 teaspoon chopped chives
- 1 teaspoon ground black pepper
- 1 teaspoon chopped thyme
- 4 tablespoons butter, unsalted, softened
- 1 teaspoon chopped rosemary
- 2 teaspoons chopped parsley

Method:

1. Take a small bowl, place butter in it, add all the herbs, and then stir until well combined.
2. Take a piece of plastic wrap, place butter mixture in it, roll the wrap into a log and then let it refrigerator for 20 minutes or more until harden.
3. Meanwhile, season the steak with salt and black pepper until coated on both sides.
4. Then Plugin the GoWise Air Fryer Oven, turn it on, insert the drip pan, and then press the menu button to select "steak"; make sure the door of the oven is closed.
5. Press the temp button, press the +/- button to adjust the temperature to 350 degrees F, press the time button, and then press the +/- button to adjust the cooking time to 5 minutes and let the air fryer oven preheat.
6. Meanwhile, take the Rotisserie Steak Cage and place the marinated steak in it.
7. Arrange the Rotisserie Steak Cage into the air fryer oven, shut the door, press the time button, press the +/- button to adjust the cooking time to 15 minutes, and let it cook until cooked to desired doneness.
8. When done, serve the steak with herb butter.

Nutrition Value:

- Calories: 260 Cal
- Fat: 18 g
- Carbs: 2 g
- Protein: 23 g
- Fiber: 0.5 g

Steak Fajitas

Preparation time: 10 minutes
Cooking time: 10 minutes
Servings: 4

Ingredients:

- 1 large red bell pepper, cored, sliced
- ½ of a medium yellow onion, peeled, sliced
- 2 chopped serrano peppers
- ½ of a medium red onion, peeled, sliced
- ¼ teaspoon garlic powder
- 1 pound sliced beef
- 2 teaspoons salt
- ½ teaspoon ground cumin
- 1 teaspoon ground black pepper
- ¼ teaspoon dried oregano
- ¼ teaspoon red chili powder
- 2 tablespoons olive oil

Method:

1. Plugin the GoWise Air Fryer Oven, turn it on, insert the drip pan and parchment-lined wire rack, and then press the menu button to select "steak"; make sure the door of the oven is closed.
2. Press the temp button, and then press the +/- button to adjust the temperature to 350 degrees F, press the time button, and then press the +/- button to adjust the cooking time to 5 minutes and let the air fryer oven preheat.
3. Meanwhile, take a large bowl, place onions and peppers in it, add steak strips, add remaining ingredients and then toss until well coated.
4. Spread beef and vegetables on the wire rack, shut the door, press the time button, press the +/- button to adjust the cooking time to 10 minutes, and let it cook until don't, tossing halfway.
5. Serve steak fajitas with taco chips.

Nutrition Value:

- Calories: 153 Cal
- Fat: 5 g
- Carbs: 1 g
- Protein: 25 g
- Fiber: 0.3 g

Philly Cheesesteak

Preparation time: 15 minutes
Cooking time: 17 minutes
Servings: 2

Ingredients:

- 12 ounces of rib-eye steak, cut into thin slices
- ½ of a small white onion, peeled, sliced
- ½ of medium green bell pepper, cored, sliced
- 1 teaspoon salt
- ½ teaspoon Worcestershire sauce
- 1 teaspoon ground black pepper
- ½ teaspoon soy sauce
- 1 tablespoon olive oil
- 2 slices of provolone cheese, halved
- 2 rolls

Method:

1. Plugin the GoWise Air Fryer Oven, turn it on, insert the parchment-lined wire rack, and then press the menu button to select "steak"; make sure the door of the oven is closed.
2. Press the temp button, and then press the +/- button to adjust the temperature to 400 degrees F, press the time button, and then press the +/- button to adjust the cooking time to 5 minutes and let the air fryer oven preheat.
3. Meanwhile, take a medium bowl, place steak slices in it, add ½ teaspoon salt, ½ teaspoon black pepper, soy sauce, and Worcestershire sauce and then toss until coated, set aside until required.
4. Take a separate medium bowl, place onion and green bell pepper slices, drizzle with oil, season with remaining salt and black pepper and then toss until coated.
5. Spread steak slices and vegetable slices on the wire rack, press the time button, press the +/- button to adjust the cooking time to 15 minutes, and let it cook, tossing halfway.
6. Cut each roll in half, split it lengthwise, top with cooked steak and vegetable mixture, and then top with cheese.
7. Arrange the sandwiches on the wire rack, and then air-fry for 2 minutes until cheese melts.
8. Serve straight away.

Nutrition Value:

- Calories: 376 Cal
- Fat: 23 g
- Carbs: 18 g
- Protein: 23.5 g
- Fiber: 1 g

Mummy Hotdogs

Preparation time: 15 minutes
Cooking time: 10 minutes
Servings: 10

Ingredients:

- 10 hot dogs
- 1 can of crescent dough rolls
- 3 slices of American cheese
- ¼ cup mustard paste

Method:

1. Plugin the GoWise Air Fryer Oven, turn it on, insert the wire rack, and then press the menu button to select "manual"; make sure the door of the oven is closed.
2. Press the temp button, and then press the +/- button to adjust the temperature to 390 degrees F, press the time button, and then press the +/- button to adjust the cooking time to 5 minutes and let the air fryer oven preheat.
3. Meanwhile, unroll the dough, make a large rectangle of its perforations, press to seal so that there are no holes and then cut the dough into ½-inch thick pieces.
4. Cut the cheese into ½-inch thick slices, place a cheese piece on a hot dog
5. wrap with a dough piece like a bandage, and then repeat with the remaining hot dogs.
6. Arrange the prepared hot dogs on the wire rack, shut the door of the air fryer oven, press the time button, press the +/- button to adjust the cooking time to 10 minutes, and let it cook until nicely golden brown, turning halfway.
7. When done, make eyes on each hot dog mummy by pipping mustard on it and then serve.

Nutrition Value:

- Calories: 330 Cal
- Fat: 27 g
- Carbs: 11 g
- Protein: 11 g
- Fiber: 2 g

Chapter 4: Pork

Garlic and Herb Pork Chops

Preparation time: 10 minutes
Cooking time: 20 minutes
Servings: 4

Ingredients:

- 4 pork chops, bone-in
- ¼ cup chopped parsley
- 2 teaspoons chopped rosemary
- 1 ½ teaspoon sea salt
- 1 lemon, zested
- 3 tablespoons olive oil

Method:

1. Plugin the GoWise Air Fryer Oven, turn it on, insert the drip pan/ wire rack/ mesh basket/ mesh rack, and then press the menu button to select "manual"; make sure the door of the oven is closed.
2. Press the temp button, and then press the +/- button to adjust the temperature to 400 degrees F, press the time button, and then press the +/- button to adjust the cooking time to 5 minutes and let the air fryer oven preheat.
3. Meanwhile, prepare the pork chops and for this, season them with rosemary and ½ teaspoon salt until coated.
4. Place two pork chops into the Rotisserie Steak Cage, insert it into the air fryer oven, and then shut its door.
5. Press the time button, press the +/- button to adjust the cooking time to 10 minutes and let it cook.
6. Meanwhile, prepare herb mixture and for this, take a small bowl, place remaining ingredients in it, and then stir until mixed.
7. When pork chops have cooked, transfer them onto a plate, and then cook the remaining pork chops in the same manner.
8. Drizzle the prepared herb mixture over the pork chops and then serve.

Nutrition Value:

- Calories: 429.6 Cal
- Fat: 28.1 g
- Carbs: 0.3 g
- Protein: 41.3 g
- Fiber: 0.2 g

Salt and Pepper Pork Belly

Preparation time: 10 minutes
Cooking time: 15 minutes
Servings: 4

Ingredients:

- 1 pound pork belly slices
- 1 teaspoon of sea salt
- 4 tablespoons olive oil
- ½ teaspoon ground black pepper

Method:

1. Plugin the GoWise Air Fryer Oven, turn it on, insert the drip pan with wire rack, and then press the menu button to select "manual"; make sure the door of the oven is closed.
2. Press the temp button, and then press the +/- button to adjust the temperature to 390 degrees F, press the time button, and then press the +/- button to adjust the cooking time to 5 minutes and let the air fryer oven preheat.
3. Meanwhile, cut pork belly slices into strips, place them in a large bowl, add salt, black pepper, and oil and then toss until coated.
4. Arrange the pork belly strips on the wire rack in the single, shut the door of the air fryer oven, press the time button, press the +/- button to adjust the cooking time to 15 minutes, and let it cook.
5. Serve straight away.

Nutrition Value:

- Calories: 332 Cal
- Fat: 24 g
- Carbs: 0 g
- Protein: 26 g
- Fiber: 0 g

Pork Bites with Mushrooms

Preparation time: 10 minutes
Cooking time: 23 minutes
Servings: 4

Ingredients:

- 1 pound pork belly
- ½ teaspoon garlic powder
- 8 ounces mushrooms, halved
- 1 teaspoon salt
- ½ teaspoon ground black pepper
- 1 teaspoon Worcestershire sauce
- 2 tablespoons butter, melted

Method:

1. Plugin the GoWise Air Fryer Oven, turn it on, insert the drip pan with wire rack, and then press the menu button to select "manual"; make sure the door of the oven is closed.
2. Press the temp button, and then press the +/- button to adjust the temperature to 400 degrees F, press the time button, and then press the +/- button to adjust the cooking time to 5 minutes and let the air fryer oven preheat.
3. Meanwhile, cut the pork chops into ¾-inch thick cubes, and then place them in a large bowl.
4. Add mushrooms, butter, salt, black pepper, garlic powder, and Worcestershire, and then toss until well combined.
5. Spread pork and mushrooms mixture on the wire rack, shut the door of the air fryer oven, press the time button, press the +/- button to adjust the cooking time to 23 minutes, and let it cook, tossing halfway.
6. Serve straight away.

Nutrition Value:

- Calories: 241 Cal
- Fat: 14 g
- Carbs: 2 g
- Protein: 26 g
- Fiber: 1 g

Pork Chops

Preparation time: 10 minutes
Cooking time: 30 minutes
Servings: 2

Ingredients:

- 2 pork chops, center-cut, bone-in, about 2 inches thick
- ½ teaspoon onion powder
- ¼ teaspoon garlic powder
- 1 teaspoon ground mustard
- 1 ½ teaspoons salt
- 1 tablespoon paprika
- 1 ½ teaspoons ground black pepper
- 2 tablespoons brown sugar
- 2 tablespoons olive oil

Method:

1. Plugin the GoWise Air Fryer Oven, turn it on, insert the drip pan and then press the menu button to select "manual"; make sure the door of the oven is closed.
2. Press the temp button, and then press the +/- button to adjust the temperature to 400 degrees F, press the time button, and then press the +/- button to adjust the cooking time to 5 minutes and let the air fryer oven preheat.
3. Meanwhile, take a small bowl, place all the spices and seasonings and then stir until mixed.
4. Brush the pork chops with oil and then rub with prepared spice mix until coated.
5. Place a pork chop into the Rotisserie Steak Cage, insert it into the air fryer oven, and then shut its door.
6. Press the time button, press the +/- button to adjust the cooking time to 15 minutes and let it cook.
7. Serve straight away.

Nutrition Value:

- Calories: 209.4 Cal
- Fat: 11.1 g
- Carbs: 5.5 g
- Protein: 21.1 g
- Fiber: 1 g

Baby Back Ribs

Preparation time: 10 minutes
Cooking time: 40 minutes
Servings: 4

Ingredients:

- 2 tablespoons olive oil
- 1 rack of baby back ribs, cut into sections

For the Seasoning:

- 1 teaspoon onion powder
- 2 teaspoons salt
- ½ teaspoon garlic powder
- 1 teaspoon ground black pepper
- ½ teaspoon brown sugar
- 1 teaspoon red chili powder

Method:

1. Plugin the GoWise Air Fryer Oven, turn it on, insert the drip pan with a wire rack, and then press the menu button to select "manual"; make sure the door of the oven is closed.
2. Press the temp button, and then press the +/- button to adjust the temperature to 400 degrees F, press the time button, and then press the +/- button to adjust the cooking time to 5 minutes and let the air fryer oven preheat.
3. Meanwhile, take a small bowl, place all the ingredients for the seasonings in it, stir until combined, and then rub this mixture on all sides of the ribs section.
4. Arrange the seasoned ribs on the wire rack, shut the door of the air fryer oven, press the time button, press the +/- button to adjust the cooking time to 40 minutes, and let it cook.
5. Serve straight away.

Nutrition Value:

- Calories: 269 Cal
- Fat: 20 g
- Carbs: 1.5 g
- Protein: 27 g
- Fiber: 0 g

Pork Chops with Broccoli

Preparation time: 10 minutes
Cooking time: 12 minutes
Servings: 2

Ingredients:

- 2 bone-in pork chops, each about 5 ounces
- 2 cups broccoli florets
- ½ teaspoon onion powder
- 1 teaspoon minced garlic
- ½ teaspoon garlic powder
- 1 teaspoon salt, divided
- ½ teaspoon paprika
- 2 tablespoons avocado oil, divided

Method:

1. Plugin the GoWise Air Fryer Oven, turn it on, insert the drip pan with wire rack, and then press the menu button to select "manual"; make sure the door of the oven is closed.
2. Press the temp button, and then press the +/- button to adjust the temperature to 350 degrees F, press the time button, and then press the +/- button to adjust the cooking time to 5 minutes and let the air fryer oven preheat.
3. Meanwhile, brush the pork chops with 1 tablespoon of oil and then season with ½ tablespoon salt, garlic powder, onion powder, and paprika.
4. Arrange the seasoned pork chops on the wire rack, shut the door of the air fryer oven, press the time button, press the +/- button to adjust the cooking time to 7 minutes, and let it cook.
5. Meanwhile, take a medium bowl, place broccoli florets in it, add remaining oil, minced garlic, and remaining salt and then toss until coated.
6. After 7 minutes, spread broccoli florets on the wire rack and then continue air frying for 5 minutes until done, tossing broccoli florets halfway.
7. Serve straight away.

Nutrition Value:

- Calories: 483 Cal
- Fat: 30 g
- Carbs: 12 g
- Protein: 40 g
- Fiber: 6 g

Breaded Pork Chops

Preparation time: 10 minutes
Cooking time: 25 minutes
Servings: 4

Ingredients:

- 1 pound boneless pork chops, each about ½ inch thick
- ½ cup all-purpose flour
- 1 teaspoon onion powder, divided
- ½ teaspoon salt
- 1 teaspoon garlic powder, divided
- 1/3 cup seasoned Italian breadcrumbs
- ¼ teaspoon ground black pepper
- 2 eggs
- 1/3 cup grated parmesan cheese

Method:

1. Plugin the GoWise Air Fryer Oven, turn it on, insert the drip pan with a wire rack, and then press the menu button to select "manual"; make sure the door of the oven is closed.
2. Press the temp button, and then press the +/- button to adjust the temperature to 400 degrees F, press the time button, and then press the +/- button to adjust the cooking time to 5 minutes and let the air fryer oven preheat.
3. Meanwhile, take a shallow dish, place flour in it, add ½ teaspoon each of onion and garlic powder, and then stir until mixed.
4. Take a separate shallow dish, crack eggs in it, add remaining onion powder and garlic powder, and then whisk until combined.
5. Take a separate shallow dish, place breadcrumbs in it, add cheese and then stir until mixed.
6. Working on one pork chop at a time, dredge it in flour mixture, dip into egg and then dredge into the breadcrumbs mixture until coated.
7. Place two pork chops into the Rotisserie Steak Cage, insert it into the air fryer oven, and then shut its door.
8. Press the time button, press the +/- button to adjust the cooking time to 12 minutes and let it cook.
9. Serve straight away.

Nutrition Value:

- Calories: 347 Cal
- Fat: 13 g
- Carbs: 20 g
- Protein: 34 g
- Fiber: 1 g

Chapter 5: Seafood

Bacon-Wrapped Shrimp

Preparation time: 10 minutes
Cooking time: 4 minutes
Servings: 4

Ingredients:

- 12 slices of bacon
- 12 large shrimps, peeled, deveined
- ½ of a lemon, juiced

Method:

1. Plugin the GoWise Air Fryer Oven, turn it on, insert the drip pan and wire rack, and then press the menu button to select "manual"; make sure the door of the oven is closed.
2. Press the temp button, and then press the +/- button to adjust the temperature to 350 degrees F, press the time button, and then press the +/- button to adjust the cooking time to 5 minutes and let the air fryer oven preheat.
3. Meanwhile, take a large bowl, place shrimps in it, add lemon juice and then toss until coated.
4. Wrap each shrimp with a bacon slice, arrange it on the wire rack, and then shut the door of the air fryer oven.
5. Press the time button, press the +/- button to adjust the cooking time to 4 minutes and let it cook.
6. Serve straight away.

Nutrition Value:

- Calories: 207.6 Cal
- Fat: 2 g
- Carbs: 1 g
- Protein: 23 g
- Fiber: 0 g

Shrimp Fajitas

Preparation time: 10 minutes
Cooking time: 12 minutes
Servings: 4

Ingredients:

- 1 pound shrimp, peeled, deveined
- ½ of a small white onion, peeled, sliced
- 1 medium green bell pepper, cored, sliced
- 1 large poblano chili
- 1 medium yellow bell pepper, cored, sliced
- 1 teaspoon minced garlic
- 1 jalapeno, sliced
- 4 tablespoons fajita seasoning
- 2 tablespoons lime juice
- 4 tablespoons olive oil

Method:

1. Plugin the GoWise Air Fryer Oven, turn it on, insert the parchment lined wire rack, and then press the menu button to select "manual"; make sure the door of the oven is closed.
2. Press the temp button, and then press the +/- button to adjust the temperature to 370 degrees F, press the time button, and then press the +/- button to adjust the cooking time to 5 minutes and let the air fryer oven preheat.
3. Meanwhile, take a large bowl, place all the ingredients in it and then toss until thoroughly combined.
4. Spread shrimps and vegetable mixture on the wire rack, shut the door of the air fryer oven, press the time button, press the +/- button to adjust the cooking time to 12 minutes, and let it cook until done, turning halfway.
5. Serve straight away.

Nutrition Value:

- Calories: 262.8 Cal
- Fat: 10.2 g
- Carbs: 27 g
- Protein: 15.8 g
- Fiber: 2.2 g

Breaded Fried Shrimp

Preparation time: 10 minutes
Cooking time: 8 minutes
Servings: 4

Ingredients:

For the Shrimps:

- ½ cup all-purpose flour
- 1 pound shrimp, peeled, deveined
- 1 teaspoons salt
- 1 tablespoon chicken seasoning
- ½ teaspoon ground black pepper
- 1 teaspoon paprika
- ¾ cup panko bread crumbs
- 1 egg white

For the Sauce:

- ¼ cup sweet chili sauce
- 2 tablespoons Sriracha
- 1/3 cup Greek yogurt

Method:

1. Plugin the GoWise Air Fryer Oven, turn it on, insert the drip pan and wire rack, and then press the menu button to select "manual"; make sure the door of the oven is closed.
2. Press the temp button, and then press the +/- button to adjust the temperature to 400 degrees F, press the time button, and then press the +/- button to adjust the cooking time to 5 minutes and let the air fryer oven preheat.
3. Meanwhile, prepare the shrimps and for this, place them in a large bowl, add salt, black pepper, paprika, and chicken seasoning and then toss until coated.
4. Take a shallow dish and then place flour in it.
5. Take a separate shallow dish and then place egg white in it.
6. Take another separate shallow dish and then place breadcrumbs in it.
7. Working on one shrimp at a time, dredge in flour, dab in egg white, and then coat in breadcrumbs.
8. Arrange the shrimps on the wire rack, shut the door of the air fryer oven, press the time button, press the +/- button to adjust the cooking time to 8 minutes, and let it cook until done.
9. Meanwhile, prepare the sauce and for this, take a medium bowl, place all of its ingredients in it and then whisk until combined, set aside until required.
10. Serve the shrimps with prepared sauce.

Nutrition Value:

- Calories: 242 Cal
- Fat: 1 g
- Carbs: 32 g
- Protein: 37 g
- Fiber: 4 g

Low Country Boil Skewers

Preparation time: 15 minutes
Cooking time: 30 minutes
Servings: 6

Ingredients:

- 10 large shrimp, peeled, deveined
- 6 baby red potatoes
- 8 ounces smoked pork sausage
- 1 ear of corn, cut into 1-inch rounds
- 1 teaspoon salt
- 1 tablespoon minced garlic
- 2 tablespoons crab boil seasoning
- 2 teaspoons hot sauce
- 4 tablespoons butter, unsalted
- 1 teaspoon apple cider vinegar

Method:

1. Take a medium saucepan, place baby potatoes in it, pour in enough water to cover them, and then stir in 1 tablespoon crab boil seasoning and salt.
2. Place the saucepan over medium-high heat, bring to boil, and then simmer for 7 minutes.
3. Cut corn into ½-inch thick rounds, add to the saucepan, and then continue cooking for 5 minutes until cooked.
4. When done, drain potatoes and corn into a colander and let them cool.
5. Take a small skillet pan, place it over medium heat, add butter, and then let it melt.
6. Add garlic, cook for 1 minute until fragrant, stir in vinegar and hot sauce, remove the pan from heat and then reserve half of this mixture.
7. Plugin the GoWise Air Fryer Oven, turn it on, insert the drip pan, and then press the menu button to select "manual"; make sure the door of the oven is closed.
8. Press the temp button, and then press the +/- button to adjust the temperature to 320 degrees F, press the time button, and then press the +/- button to adjust the cooking time to 5 minutes and let the air fryer oven preheat.
9. Thread potatoes, corn, sausage, and shrimps into the Rotisserie Skewers, and then brush with half of the sauce mixture.
10. Arrange the skewers into the air fryer oven, shut with its door, press the time button, press the +/- button to adjust the cooking time to 10 minutes, and let it cook.
11. Serve straight away.

Nutrition Value:

- Calories: 78 Cal
- Fat: 4 g

- Carbs: 6 g
- Protein: 5 g
- Fiber: 0.7 g

Shrimp and Sausage Veggie Skewers

Preparation time: 10 minutes
Cooking time: 5 minutes
Servings: 6

Ingredients:

- 1 pound shrimps, peeled, deveined
- 1 medium red bell pepper, cored, cut into chunks
- 2 medium zucchini, sliced
- 1 medium yellow bell pepper, cored, cut into chunks
- 14 ounces of pork sausage, sliced
- 1 teaspoon salt
- 1 tablespoon Cajun seasoning
- 1 teaspoon ground black pepper
- 3 tablespoons olive oil

Method:

1. Plugin the GoWise Air Fryer Oven, turn it on, insert the drip pan, and then press the menu button to select "manual"; make sure the door of the oven is closed.
2. Press the temp button, and then press the +/- button to adjust the temperature to 350 degrees F, press the time button, and then press the +/- button to adjust the cooking time to 5 minutes and let the air fryer oven preheat.
3. Meanwhile, take a large bowl, place shrimps in it, add bell peppers, zucchini, and sausage, season with salt, black pepper, and Cajun seasoning
4. drizzle with oil and then toss until coated.
5. Thread bell pepper, zucchini, sausage, and shrimp into the Rotisserie Skewers, arrange the skewers into the air fryer oven, shut with its door, press the time button, press the +/- button to adjust the cooking time to 5 minutes, and let it cook until shrimps turn opaque.
6. Serve straight away.

Nutrition Value:

- Calories: 142.1 Cal
- Fat: 3.6 g
- Carbs: 5.7 g
- Protein: 20.8 g
- Fiber: 1.1 g

Garlic Shrimp

Preparation time: 10 minutes
Cooking time: 15 minutes
Servings: 4

Ingredients:

- 1 pound shrimps, peeled, deveined
- ¼ teaspoon garlic powder
- 1 teaspoon salt
- 1 teaspoon ground black pepper
- ½ teaspoon red chili flakes
- 2 tablespoons olive oil
- 1 lemon, juiced

Method:

1. Plugin the GoWise Air Fryer Oven, turn it on, insert the drip pan with wire rack, and then press the menu button to select "manual"; make sure the door of the oven is closed.
2. Press the temp button, and then press the +/- button to adjust the temperature to 400 degrees F, press the time button, and then press the +/- button to adjust the cooking time to 5 minutes and let the air fryer oven preheat.
3. Meanwhile, take a large bowl, place shrimps in it, add remaining ingredients and then toss until coated.
4. Arrange the shrimps on the wire rack, shut the door of the air fryer oven, press the time button, press the +/- button to adjust the cooking time to 15 minutes, and let it cook until done, flipping halfway.
5. Drizzle juiced over the shrimps and then serve.

Nutrition Value:

- Calories: 228 Cal
- Fat: 3 g
- Carbs: 1 g
- Protein: 46 g
- Fiber: 0 g

Garlic Parmesan Shrimps

Preparation time: 10 minutes
Cooking time: 10 minutes
Servings: 4

Ingredients:

- 1 pound shrimp, peeled, deveined
- 3 teaspoons minced garlic
- 1 tablespoon lemon juice
- 1 teaspoon salt
- 1 teaspoon ground black pepper
- 1 tablespoon olive oil
- ½ cup grated parmesan cheese

Method:

1. Take a large bowl, place shrimps in it, add salt, black pepper, garlic, lemon juice, and oil and then toss until coated.
2. Cover the bowl with a plastic wrap, place it into the refrigerator, and then let it marinate for 1 hour.
3. Then Plugin the GoWise Air Fryer Oven, turn it on, insert the drip pan and wire rack, and then press the menu button to select "manual"; make sure the door of the oven is closed.
4. Press the temp button, and then press the +/- button to adjust the temperature to 350 degrees F, press the time button, and then press the +/- button to adjust the cooking time to 5 minutes and let the air fryer oven preheat.
5. Meanwhile, remove the bowl from the refrigerator, uncover it, add cheese and then toss until mixed.
6. Arrange the shrimps on the wire rack, shut the door of the air fryer oven and press the time button, press the +/- button to adjust the cooking time to 10 minutes, and let it cook until shrimps turn opaque.
7. Serve straight away.

Nutrition Value:

- Calories: 151 Cal
- Fat: 6 g
- Carbs: 4 g
- Protein: 20 g
- Fiber: 0 g

Chapter 6: Fish

Pecan Crusted Halibut

Preparation time: 10 minutes
Cooking time: 10 minutes
Servings: 4

Ingredients:

- 4 halibut fillets, skinless, each about 4 ounces
- ½ cup pecan pieces
- 2 tablespoons lemon pepper seasoning
- divided
- ½ cup cornstarch
- ½ cup panko breadcrumbs
- ½ cup white wine
- 2 egg whites

Method:

1. Plugin the GoWise Air Fryer Oven, turn it on, insert the drip pan with a wire rack, and then press the menu button to select "fish"; make sure the door of the oven is closed.
2. Press the temp button, and then press the +/- button to adjust the temperature to 375 degrees F, press the time button, and then press the +/- button to adjust the cooking time to 5 minutes and let the air fryer oven preheat.
3. Meanwhile, take a shallow dish, place egg whites in it, add cornstarch, and then whisk until blended.
4. Slowly whisk in wine until combined, and then whisk in 1 teaspoon lemon pepper seasoning until mixed.
5. Place pecans into a food processor, pulse until mixture resembles crumbs, tip into a shallow dish, add breadcrumbs, and then stir until combined.
6. Season the fillets with salt and remaining lemon pepper seasoning
7. dip into the egg mixture and then dredge into the pecan mixture until well coated.
8. Arrange the fillets on the wire rack, shut the door of the air fryer oven, press the time button, press the +/- button to adjust the cooking time to 10 minutes, and let it cook until done.
9. Serve straight away.

Nutrition Value:

- Calories: 432 Cal
- Fat: 16 g
- Carbs: 31 g
- Protein: 37 g

- Fiber: 3 g

Beer Battered Fish

Preparation time: 10 minutes
Cooking time: 15 minutes
Servings: 4

Ingredients:

- 1 pound cod, cut into large pieces
- 1 ½ cups all-purpose flour
- 1 teaspoon salt
- ½ tablespoon red chili powder
- ½ teaspoon ground black pepper
- 1 tablespoon ground cumin
- 1 ½ cups cornstarch
- 2 eggs
- 10 ounces Mexican beer

Method:

1. Plugin the GoWise Air Fryer Oven, turn it on, insert the drip pan with a wire rack, and then press the menu button to select "fish"; make sure the door of the oven is closed.
2. Press the temp button, and then press the +/- button to adjust the temperature to 375 degrees F, press the time button, and then press the +/- button to adjust the cooking time to 5 minutes and let the air fryer oven preheat.
3. Meanwhile, take a shallow dish, crack eggs in it, pour in beer, whisk until blended, and then set aside until required.
4. Take a separate shallow dish, place flour in it, add salt, black pepper, red chili powder, cumin, and cornstarch and then stir until mixed.
5. Working on one piece of fish, dip into the beer mixture, and then dredge in flour until coated.
6. Arrange the coated fish pieces on the wire rack, shut the door of the air fryer oven, press the time button, press the +/- button to adjust the cooking time to 15 minutes, and let it cook until done, turning halfway.
7. Serve straight away.

Nutrition Value:

- Calories: 245 Cal
- Fat: 22.5 g
- Carbs: 21 g
- Protein: 14 g
- Fiber: 0.5 g

Crumbed Fish

Preparation time: 10 minutes
Cooking time: 12 minutes
Servings: 4

Ingredients:

- 4 fillets of founder
- 1 lemon, sliced
- 1 cup panko breadcrumbs
- 1 egg
- ¼ cup olive oil

Method:

1. Plugin the GoWise Air Fryer Oven, turn it on, insert the drip pan with a wire rack, and then press the menu button to select "fish"; make sure the door of the oven is closed.
2. Press the temp button, and then press the +/- button to adjust the temperature to 350 degrees F, press the time button, and then press the +/- button to adjust the cooking time to 5 minutes and let the air fryer oven preheat.
3. Meanwhile, take a shallow dish, place bread crumbs in it, add oil and then stir until well mixed.
4. Working on one fillet at a time, dip into the bread crumbs mixture until coated, and then arrange on the wire rack.
5. Press the time button, press the +/- button to adjust the cooking time to 12 minutes and let it cook until done.
6. Serve straight away.

Nutrition Value:

- Calories: 354.1 Cal
- Fat: 17.7 g
- Carbs: 22.5 g
- Protein: 26.9 g
- Fiber: 2.5 g

Tuna Melts

Preparation time: 10 minutes
Cooking time: 5 minutes
Servings: 2

Ingredients:

- 12 ounces canned tuna
- ¼ of a medium white onion, peeled, chopped
- 2 dill pickles
- ½ teaspoon garlic Powder
- ½ teaspoon ground Black Pepper
- 4 slices of American cheese
- ¼ cup mayonnaise
- 4 slices of bread

Method:

1. Plugin the GoWise Air Fryer Oven, turn it on, insert the wire rack, and then press the menu button to select "fish"; make sure the door of the oven is closed.
2. Press the temp button, and then press the +/- button to adjust the temperature to 400 degrees F, press the time button, and then press the +/- button to adjust the cooking time to 5 minutes and let the air fryer oven preheat.
3. Meanwhile, take a large bowl, place tuna in it, add onion, pickles, garlic powder, black pepper, and mayonnaise, and then stir until mixed.
4. Spread the tuna mixture on top of four bread slices, top tuna mixture with a cheese slice, and then place on the wire rack.
5. Shut the air fryer oven with its door, press the time button, press the +/- button to adjust the cooking time to 5 minutes, and let it cook.
6. Serve straight away.

Nutrition Value:

- Calories: 275.5 Cal
- Fat: 12.5 g
- Carbs: 21.5 g
- Protein: 18 g
- Fiber: 0.8 g

Salmon

Preparation time: 10 minutes
Cooking time: 10 minutes
Servings: 1

Ingredients:

- 1 fillet of salmon
- ½ teaspoon garlic powder
- ½ teaspoon salt
- ½ teaspoon smoked paprika
- 1 teaspoon olive oil

Method:

1. Plugin the GoWise Air Fryer Oven, turn it on, insert the drip pan with a wire rack, and then press the menu button to select "fish"; make sure the door of the oven is closed.
2. Press the temp button, and then press the +/- button to adjust the temperature to 400 degrees F, press the time button, and then press the +/- button to adjust the cooking time to 5 minutes and let the air fryer oven preheat.
3. Meanwhile, brush oil over salmon and then season with salt, paprika, and garlic powder until coated.
4. Arrange salmon on the wire rack, shut the door of the air fryer oven, press the time button, press the +/- button to adjust the cooking time to 10 minutes, and let it cook until done.
5. Serve straight away.

Nutrition Value:

- Calories: 274 Cal
- Fat: 19 g
- Carbs: 1 g
- Protein: 24 g
- Fiber: 0.5 g

Fish Cakes

Preparation time: 10 minutes
Cooking time: 10 minutes
Servings: 2

Ingredients:

- 10 ounces chopped cod
- ⅛ teaspoon salt
- 3 tablespoons chopped cilantro
- ¼ teaspoon ground black pepper
- 2 tablespoons Thai sweet chili sauce
- 2/3 cup whole-wheat panko breadcrumbs
- 2 tablespoons mayonnaise
- 1 egg
- 2 wedges of lime

Method:

1. Plugin the GoWise Air Fryer Oven, turn it on, insert the drip pan and parchment-lined wire rack, and then press the menu button to select "fish"; make sure the door of the oven is closed.
2. Press the temp button, and then press the +/- button to adjust the temperature to 400 degrees F, press the time button, and then press the +/- button to adjust the cooking time to 5 minutes and let the air fryer oven preheat.
3. Meanwhile, take a large bowl, place all the ingredients in it, stir until combined, and then shape the mixture into four patties, each about 3-inch.
4. Arrange the fish cakes on the wire rack, shut the door of the air fryer oven, press the time button, press the +/- button to adjust the cooking time to 10 minutes, and let it cook until done, turning halfway.
5. Serve straight away.

Nutrition Value:

- Calories: 399 Cal
- Fat: 15.5 g
- Carbs: 28 g
- Protein: 34.6 g
- Fiber: 2.8 g

Chapter 7: Vegetarian

Kale Chips

Preparation time: 10 minutes
Cooking time: 12 minutes
Servings: 2

Ingredients:

- 1 pound kale
- 1 teaspoon of sea salt
- 1 tablespoon olive oil

Method:

1. Plugin the GoWise Air Fryer Oven, turn it on, insert the parchment-lined wire rack, and then press the menu button to select "vegetables"; make sure the door of the oven is closed.
2. Press the temp button, press the +/- button to adjust the temperature to 400 degrees F, press the time button, and then press the +/- button to adjust the cooking time to 5 minutes and let the air fryer oven preheat.
3. Meanwhile, cut off the kale stem and then cut the kale leaves into bite-size pieces.
4. Take a large bowl, place kale leaves into it, add salt and oil, and then toss until coated.
5. Spread kale leaves on the wire rack in a single layer, shut the door of the air fryer oven, press the time button, press the +/- button to adjust the cooking time to 3 minutes, and let it cook until done.
6. Repeat with the remaining kale chips and then serve.

Nutrition Value:

- Calories: 110 Cal
- Fat: 4.6 g
- Carbs: 15.8 g
- Protein: 5.3 g
- Fiber: 5.6 g

Italian Breaded Eggplant

Preparation time: 35 minutes
Cooking time: 17 minutes
Servings: 6

Ingredients:

- ½ cup almond flour
- 1 medium eggplant, sliced into rounds
- 1 teaspoon salt
- 1 cup Italian breadcrumbs
- ¼ cup olive oil
- 2 eggs
- 2 cups spaghetti sauce
- 1 pound mozzarella cheese, sliced into rounds

Method:

1. Take a baking sheet, line it with a paper towel, arrange eggplant slices on it, sprinkle salt on both sides and then let it rest for 20 minutes.
2. Then Plugin the GoWise Air Fryer Oven, turn it on, insert the parchment-lined wire rack, and then press the menu button to select "manual"; make sure the door of the oven is closed.
3. Press the temp button, and then press the +/- button to adjust the temperature to 350 degrees F, press the time button, and then press the +/- button to adjust the cooking time to 5 minutes and let the air fryer oven preheat.
4. Meanwhile, take a shallow dish, place flour in it, take a separate shallow dish, crack the eggs in it and then whisk until blended.
5. Take another separate shallow dish, place breadcrumbs in it, add oil and then stir until mixed.
6. Working on one eggplant slice at a time, dredge in flour, dip into the egg and then dredge in breadcrumbs mixture until coated.
7. Arrange the eggplant slices on the wire rack, shut the door of the air fryer oven, press the time button, press the +/- button to adjust the cooking time to 12 minutes, and let it cook until done, flipping halfway.
8. When done, coat the eggplant slices with spaghetti sauce, top with cheese round, and then continue air frying for 5 minutes.
9. Serve straight away.

Nutrition Value:

- Calories: 116.7 Cal
- Fat: 2.2 g
- Carbs: 20.3 g
- Protein: 5 g
- Fiber: 4.1 g

Cauliflower Pizza Crust

Preparation time: 10 minutes
Cooking time: 18 minutes
Servings: 4

Ingredients:

For the Crust:

- 1 medium head of cauliflower, cut into florets
- ¼ teaspoon garlic powder
- ½ teaspoon salt
- ½ teaspoon dried oregano
- ¼ cup grated Parmesan cheese
- 2 eggs
- ½ cup shredded mozzarella cheese

For the Toppings:

- 8 slices of pepperoni
- ½ cup shredded Mozzarella cheese
- 4 whole mushrooms, sliced
- ¼ cup Pizza sauce

Method:

1. Place cauliflower florets in a food processor and then pulse until the mixture resemble rice.
2. Place cauliflower rice into a heat-proof bowl, cover with a plastic wrap, and then microwave for 3 to 4 minutes until steamed.
3. When done, drain the cauliflower well and then place in a large bowl.
4. Add garlic powder, salt, oregano, cheeses, and egg
5. and then stir until combined.
6. Plugin the GoWise Air Fryer Oven, turn it on, insert the wire rack, and then press the menu button to select "vegetables"; make sure the door of the oven is closed.
7. Press the temp button, and then press the +/- button to adjust the temperature to 350 degrees F, press the time button, and then press the +/- button to adjust the cooking time to 5 minutes and let the air fryer oven preheat.
8. Meanwhile, take a large piece of parchment sheet, place cauliflower mixture, and then spread it into the round crust.
9. Place the cauliflower crust along with the parchment sheet on the wire rack, shut the door of the air fryer oven, press the time button, press the +/- button to adjust the cooking time to 14 minutes and let it cook.
10. Then flip for the crust, spread the pizza sauce on top, scatter pepperoni slices and mushroom slices and sprinkle cheese.

11. Return the crust into the air fryer oven and then continue air frying for 4 minutes until cheese melts.
12. Serve straight away.

Nutrition Value:

- Calories: 142.6 Cal
- Fat: 10.7 g
- Carbs: 2.6 g
- Protein: 9.5 g
- Fiber: 1.5 g

Bacon-Wrapped Brussel Sprouts

Preparation time: 10 minutes
Cooking time: 10 minutes
Servings: 4

Ingredients:

- 16 Brussel sprouts
- 8 slices of bacon
- ¼ teaspoon garlic powder
- ¼ teaspoon ground black pepper
- 1/3 cup soy sauce

Method:

1. Take a large bowl, place garlic powder and black pepper in it, pour in soy sauce, and whisk until combined.
2. Cut each Brussel sprout in half, add to the soy sauce mixture, toss until coated, then cover the bowl with its lid and let marinate for 20 minutes.
3. Plugin the GoWise Air Fryer Oven, turn it on, insert the drip pan with mesh racks and then press the menu button to select "vegetable"; make sure the door of the oven is closed.
4. Press the temp button, and then press the +/- button to adjust the temperature to 350 degrees F, press the time button, and then press the +/- button to adjust the cooking time to 5 minutes and let the air fryer oven preheat.
5. Meanwhile, take a Rotisserie Skewers, thread the end piece of bacon on it, add a Brussel sprout half, fold the bacon over it, thread another Brussel sprout half, fold the bacon over it and repeat until all the bacon and sprouts are used.
6. Arrange the skewers into the air fryer oven, shut its door, press the time button, press the +/- button to adjust the cooking time to 10 minutes, and let it cook until done.
7. Serve straight away.

Nutrition Value:

- Calories: 90 Cal
- Fat: 6 g
- Carbs: 6 g
- Protein: 6 g
- Fiber: 3 g

Sesame Cauliflower Wings

Preparation time: 10 minutes
Cooking time: 27 minutes
Servings: 2

Ingredients:

- 1 small head of cauliflower, cut into florets
- 1 cup panko breadcrumbs

For the Batter:

- ½ cup almond flour
- ½ teaspoon garlic powder
- ¼ teaspoon of sea salt
- ¼ teaspoon red pepper flakes
- ½ teaspoon ground black pepper
- 1 teaspoon sesame seeds
- 1 scallion, chopped
- ½ cup almond milk, unsweetened

For the Sauce:

- ¾ teaspoon ground ginger
- ¼ teaspoon ground black pepper
- 2 tablespoons soy sauce
- 4 tablespoons maple syrup
- ½ teaspoon sesame seeds

Method:

1. Plugin the GoWise Air Fryer Oven, turn it on, insert the drip pan with mesh racks and then press the menu button to select "vegetable"; make sure the door of the oven is closed.
2. Press the temp button, and then press the +/- button to adjust the temperature to 400 degrees F, press the time button, and then press the +/- button to adjust the cooking time to 5 minutes and let the air fryer oven preheat.
3. Meanwhile, take a shallow dish, place all the ingredients for the batter in it and then whisk until combined.
4. Take a separate shallow dish and spread breadcrumbs on it.
5. Working on one floret at a time, dip into the batter and then dredge into the breadcrumbs until coated.
6. Arrange the cauliflower florets in a single layer, shut the door of the air fryer oven, press the time button, press the +/- button to adjust the cooking time to 22 minutes, and let it cook until done.
7. Meanwhile, prepare the sauce and for this, take a medium bowl, place all of its ingredients in it and then whisk until combined, set aside until required.

8. When cauliflower florets have cooked, brush them with the prepared sauce and then continue air frying for 5 minutes.
9. Serve straight away.

Nutrition Value:

- Calories: 129 Cal
- Fat: 1 g
- Carbs: 24 g
- Protein: 7 g
- Fiber: 4 g

Roasted Garlic Hummus

Preparation time: 1 hour and 10 minutes
Cooking time: 20 minutes
Servings: 16

Ingredients:

- 2 cups cooked chickpeas
- 1 bulb of garlic
- ½ teaspoon of sea salt
- 1/8 teaspoon ground white pepper
- 2 tablespoons tahini
- 1 teaspoon lemon juice
- 5 tablespoons olive oil, divided
- 2 tablespoons water

Method:

1. Plugin the GoWise Air Fryer Oven, turn it on, insert the wire rack, and then press the menu button to select "vegetable"; make sure the door of the oven is closed.
2. Press the temp button, and then press the +/- button to adjust the temperature to 350 degrees F, press the time button, and then press the +/- button to adjust the cooking time to 5 minutes and let the air fryer oven preheat.
3. Meanwhile, separate the cloves of garlic, don't peel them, place them into a small heatproof dish, and then pour in 2 tablespoons olive oil.
4. Place the bowl on the wire rack, shut the door of the air fryer oven, press the time button, press the +/- button to adjust the cooking time to 20 minutes, and let it cook.
5. When done, remove the garlic bowl from the air fryer oven, let the garlic cool for 1 hour, and then remove the skin of each garlic clove
6. Then place chickpeas into the food processor, add garlic cloves, salt, tahini, white pepper, tahini, 1 tablespoon water, and lemon juice, and then pulse until smooth.
7. Tip the hummus into a bowl and then serve with chips or vegetable slices.

Nutrition Value:

- Calories: 70 Cal
- Fat: 6 g
- Carbs: 3 g
- Protein: 1 g
- Fiber: 1 g

Tornado Potato

Preparation time: 10 minutes
Cooking time: 45 minutes
Servings: 2

Ingredients:

- 1 large potato
- 2 tablespoons Italian bread crumbs
- ½ teaspoon salt
- 2 teaspoons paprika
- 1 teaspoon ground black pepper
- 3 tablespoons grated parmesan cheese
- 1 tablespoon olive oil

Method:

1. Plugin the GoWise Air Fryer Oven, turn it on, insert the drip pan with a wire rack, and then press the menu button to select "vegetable"; make sure the door of the oven is closed.
2. Press the temp button, and then press the +/- button to adjust the temperature to 350 degrees F, press the time button, and then press the +/- button to adjust the cooking time to 5 minutes and let the air fryer oven preheat.
3. Meanwhile, take a small bowl, place breadcrumbs, salt, black pepper, paprika, and cheese in it, and then stir until mixed.
4. Insert the potato into the Rotisserie Fork and then form spirals on it by using a paring knife and then separate the slices of spirals.
5. Drizzle oil over the potato, and then sprinkle with parmesan cheese mixture until gaps are covered.
6. Arrange the Rotisserie Fork into the air fryer oven, shut its door, press the time button, press the +/- button to adjust the cooking time to 45 minutes, and let it cook.
7. Serve straight away.

Nutrition Value:

- Calories: 212 Cal
- Fat: 15 g
- Carbs: 18.3 g
- Protein: 2.4 g
- Fiber: 1.6 g

Roasted Rainbow Vegetables

Preparation time: 10 minutes
Cooking time: 20 minutes
Servings: 4

Ingredients:

- ½ of a medium white onion, peeled, 1-inch cubed
- 1 large red bell pepper, cored, 1-inch cubed
- 1 teaspoon ground black pepper
- 1 yellow summer squash, 1-inch cubed
- 1 teaspoon salt
- 1 large zucchini, 1-inch cubed
- 1 tablespoon olive oil
- 4 ounces mushrooms, halved

Method:

1. Plugin the GoWise Air Fryer Oven, turn it on, insert the drip pan with a wire rack, and then press the menu button to select "vegetable"; make sure the door of the oven is closed.
2. Press the temp button, and then press the +/- button to adjust the temperature to 350 degrees F, press the time button, and then press the +/- button to adjust the cooking time to 5 minutes and let the air fryer oven preheat.
3. Meanwhile, take a large bowl, place all the ingredients in it and then toss until well coated.
4. Spread the vegetables on the wire rack, shut the door of the air fryer oven, press the time button, press the +/- button to adjust the cooking time to 20 minutes and let it cook until done, tossing halfway.
5. Serve straight away.

Nutrition Value:

- Calories: 69 Cal
- Fat: 3.8 g
- Carbs: 7.7 g
- Protein: 2.6 g
- Fiber: 2.3 g

Cauliflower Fritters

Preparation time: 10 minutes
Cooking time: 16 minutes
Servings: 4

Ingredients:

- 1 medium head of cauliflower, florets chopped
- 3 spring onions, chopped
- 1 tablespoon minced garlic
- 1 teaspoon salt
- ½ teaspoon ground black pepper
- 1 cup Italian breadcrumbs
- 1/3 cup of shredded cheddar cheese
- ½ cup chopped parsley
- 1/3 cup of shredded mozzarella cheese
- 1 egg

Method:

1. Plugin the GoWise Air Fryer Oven, turn it on, insert the drip pan with a parchment lined wire rack, and then press the menu button to select "vegetables"; make sure the door of the oven is closed.
2. Press the temp button, and then press the +/- button to adjust the temperature to 390 degrees F, press the time button, and then press the +/- button to adjust the cooking time to 5 minutes and let the air fryer oven preheat.
3. Meanwhile, place cauliflower florets in a food processor and then pulse until it resembles rice.
4. Tip the cauliflower rice in a bowl, add remaining ingredients, stir until combined, and then shape the mixture into sixteen patties.
5. Arrange the patties on the wire rack in a single layer, spray with oil, shut the door of the air fryer oven, press the time button, press the +/- button to adjust the cooking time to 16 minutes and let it cook until done, turning halfway.
6. Serve straight away.

Nutrition Value:

- Calories: 126 Cal
- Fat: 7.2 g
- Carbs: 4.8 g
- Protein: 10.6 g
- Fiber: 2 g

Asian Tofu Salad

Preparation time: 15 minutes
Cooking time: 15 minutes
Servings: 4

Ingredients:

For the Tofu:

- 1 teaspoon minced garlic
- 12 ounces tofu, extra-firm, pressed, drained, cubed
- 1 teaspoon grated ginger
- 1 tablespoon olive oil
- 1 tablespoon soy sauce
- ½ teaspoon Sriracha sauce

For the Salad:

- 4 cups romaine lettuce, shredded
- 1 teaspoon salt
- 1 cup carrots, sliced
- ¼ cup green onions, sliced
- 1 teaspoon ground black pepper
- 1 cup cucumber, sliced
- 1 tablespoon sugar
- 1 cup red onion, sliced
- ¼ cup of rice vinegar

Method:

1. Take a large bowl, place garlic and ginger in it, add oil, Sriracha sauce, and soy sauce, and then whisk until combined.
2. Add tofu cubes, toss until coated, cover the bowl with its lid and then let it marinate for 20 minutes.
3. Plugin the GoWise Air Fryer Oven, turn it on, insert the parchment-lined wire rack, and then press the menu button to select "manual"; make sure the door of the oven is closed.
4. Press the temp button, and then press the +/- button to adjust the temperature to 400 degrees F, press the time button, and then press the +/- button to adjust the cooking time to 5 minutes and let the air fryer oven preheat.
5. Then arrange tofu cubes on the wire rack, shut the door of the air fryer oven, press the time button, press the +/- button to adjust the cooking time to 15 minutes, and let it cook until done, turning halfway.
6. Meanwhile, prepare the salad and for this, take a large bowl, pour in vinegar, add salt, black pepper, and sugar and then whisk until sugar has dissolved.
7. Add remaining ingredients for the salad in it except for lettuce, toss until combined, and then let the salad marinate until required.

8. When tofu has cooked, add it into the salad along with lettuce, toss until combined, and then serve.

Nutrition Value:

- Calories: 285.9 Cal
- Fat: 19.8 g
- Carbs: 15.3 g
- Protein: 17.6 g
- Fiber: 4.4 g

Cauliflower Grilled Cheese

Preparation time: 10 minutes
Cooking time: 18 minutes
Servings: 2

Ingredients:

- 1 medium head of cauliflower, cut into florets
- 1 teaspoon Italian herb seasoning
- ½ cup shredded parmesan cheese
- 1 egg
- 2 thick slices of cheddar cheese

Method:

1. Plugin the GoWise Air Fryer Oven, turn it on, insert the parchment lined wire rack, and then press the menu button to select "vegetable"; make sure the door of the oven is closed.
2. Press the temp button, and then press the +/- button to adjust the temperature to 370 degrees F, press the time button, and then press the +/- button to adjust the cooking time to 5 minutes and let the air fryer oven preheat.
3. Meanwhile, place cauliflower florets in a food processor and then pulse until the mixture resembles rice.
4. Tip the cauliflower rice in a large bowl, add parmesan cheese, Italian seasoning
5. and egg
6. stir until combined, and then shape the mixture into two ¼-inch thick rectangles.
7. Arrange the cauliflower rectangles on the wire rack, shut the door of the air fryer oven, press the time button, press the +/- button to adjust the cooking time to 14 minutes, and let it cook until done, flipping halfway.
8. Then top a cheese slice on top of cauliflower rectangle and then continue air frying for 4 minutes until cheese melts.
9. Serve straight away.

Nutrition Value:

- Calories: 299.9 Cal
- Fat: 20.5 g
- Carbs: 8.9 g
- Protein: 21.8 g
- Fiber: 3.7 g

Black Bean Burger

Preparation time: 15 minutes
Cooking time: 10 minutes
Servings: 4

Ingredients:

- 2 cups cooked black beans
- ¼ cup grated white onion
- ½ teaspoon salt
- ½ teaspoon red chili powder
- ½ teaspoon ground black pepper
- ½ cup seasoned breadcrumbs
- 1 egg
- 4 leaves of lettuce
- 4 slices of tomato
- 4 tablespoons mayonnaise
- 4 hamburger buns

Method:

1. Plugin the GoWise Air Fryer Oven, turn it on, insert the parchment-lined wire rack, and then press the menu button to select "manual"; make sure the door of the oven is closed.
2. Press the temp button, and then press the +/- button to adjust the temperature to 350 degrees F, press the time button, and then press the +/- button to adjust the cooking time to 5 minutes and let the air fryer oven preheat.
3. Meanwhile, take a large bowl, place black beans in it, and then mash with a fork until broken.
4. Add onion, salt, red chili powder, black pepper, breadcrumbs, and egg
5. stir until well combined, and then shape the mixture into four patties.
6. Arrange the patties on the wire rack, spray with oil, shut the door of the air fryer oven, press the time button, press the +/- button to adjust the cooking time to 10 minutes, and let it cook until done, turning halfway.
7. Assemble the burger and for this, line the bottom half of each bun with lettuce, place a patty on it and then top with a tomato slice and 1 tablespoon mayonnaise.
8. Cover the top with the top half of the burger bun and then serve.

Nutrition Value:

- Calories: 238 Cal
- Fat: 5 g
- Carbs: 37.5 g
- Protein: 11.5 g
- Fiber: 8.5 g

Spring Rolls with Tofu

Preparation time: 10 minutes
Cooking time: 15 minutes
Servings: 6

Ingredients:

- 12 ounces tofu, extra-firm, pressed, drained, cubed
- 2 pickled radishes, sliced
- 2 green onions, sliced
- 1 bundle of cilantro, chopped
- 4 pickled carrots, sliced
- 1 tablespoon smoked paprika
- ½ cup peanut oil
- 12 rice papers of spring roll

Method:

1. Plugin the GoWise Air Fryer Oven, turn it on, insert the parchment lined wire rack, and then press the menu button to select "manual"; make sure the door of the oven is closed.
2. Press the temp button, and then press the +/- button to adjust the temperature to 370 degrees F, press the time button, and then press the +/- button to adjust the cooking time to 5 minutes and let the air fryer oven preheat.
3. Meanwhile, take a medium bowl and then pour in peanut oil.
4. Working on one tofu cube at a time, dip it into the peanut oil, arrange on the wire rack and then sprinkle with paprika.
5. Shut the door of the air fryer oven, press the time button, press the +/- button to adjust the cooking time to 15 minutes, and let it cook, flipping tofu halfway.
6. Then assemble the rolls and for this, brush the rice paper with warm water, let it rest for 5 minutes until it turns soft, and then fill it with some tofu, radish, onion, cilantro, and carrot.
7. Roll up the roll, prepared remaining rolls in the same manner, and then serve.

Nutrition Value:

- Calories: 272 Cal
- Fat: 10.4 g
- Carbs: 38 g
- Protein: 7.6 g
- Fiber: 2 g

Bacon-Wrapped Serranos

Preparation time: 10 minutes
Cooking time: 5 minutes
Servings: 4

Ingredients:

- 12 slices of cooked bacon
- 12 serrano peppers
- 2 strings of mozzarella cheeses

Method:

1. Plugin the GoWise Air Fryer Oven, turn it on, insert the parchment lined wire rack, and then press the menu button to select "manual"; make sure the door of the oven is closed.
2. Press the temp button, and then press the +/- button to adjust the temperature to 300 degrees F, press the time button, and then press the +/- button to adjust the cooking time to 5 minutes and let the air fryer oven preheat.
3. Meanwhile, cut off the stem of each pepper, make a cut on one side but don't cut all the way through, and remove seeds.
4. Stuff pepper with some cheese, wrap with a bacon slice, and then repeat with the remaining pepper.
5. Arrange the prepared peppers on the wire rack, shut the door of the air fryer oven, press the time button, press the +/- button to adjust the cooking time to 5 minutes, and let it cook.
6. Serve straight away.

Nutrition Value:

- Calories: 210 Cal
- Fat: 17 g
- Carbs: 4.5 g
- Protein: 9 g
- Fiber: 0.5 g

Stuffed Mushrooms

Preparation time: 15 minutes
Cooking time: 10 minutes
Servings: 5

Ingredients:

- 8 ounces large mushrooms
- 1 teaspoon minced garlic
- ½ teaspoon salt
- ½ teaspoon ground black pepper
- 1 teaspoon Worcestershire sauce
- 4 ounces cream cheese, softened
- 4 tablespoons shredded cheddar cheese
- ¼ cup shredded parmesan cheese

Method:

1. Plugin the GoWise Air Fryer Oven, turn it on, insert the parchment-lined wire rack, and then press the menu button to select "vegetable"; make sure the door of the oven is closed.
2. Press the temp button, and then press the +/- button to adjust the temperature to 370 degrees F, press the time button, and then press the +/- button to adjust the cooking time to 5 minutes and let the air fryer oven preheat.
3. Meanwhile, remove the stem from each mushroom and then cut off some more mushroom to make a circular area around it.
4. Take a small bowl, place cream cheese in it, microwave it for 15 seconds, and then remove it from the oven.
5. Add salt, black pepper, both cheeses, and Worcestershire sauce, stir until combined, and then stuff this mixture into the mushrooms.
6. Arrange the stuffed mushrooms on the wire rack, shut the door of the air fryer oven, press the time button, press the +/- button to adjust the cooking time to 8 minutes, and let it cook until done.
7. Serve straight away.

Nutrition Value:

- Calories: 110.3 Cal
- Fat: 7.6 g
- Carbs: 2.5 g
- Protein: 6.2 g
- Fiber: 0.6 g

French Fries

Preparation time: 10 minutes
Cooking time: 15 minutes
Servings: 6

Ingredients:

- 3 large potatoes
- 1 teaspoon salt
- ½ teaspoon ground black pepper
- 3 tablespoons olive oil

Method:

1. Peel the potatoes, cut them into fries, and then place them in a large bowl.
2. Cover the fries with water and then let them rest for 1 hour.
3. Plugin the GoWise Air Fryer Oven, turn it on, insert the drip pan with a wire rack, and then press the menu button to select "fries"; make sure the door of the oven is closed.
4. Press the temp button, and then press the +/- button to adjust the temperature to 375 degrees F, press the time button, and then press the +/- button to adjust the cooking time to 5 minutes and let the air fryer oven preheat.
5. Meanwhile, drain the potatoes, pat them dry with paper towels, and then place them in a large bowl.
6. Season potatoes with salt and black pepper, drizzle with oil, and then toss until coated.
7. Spread the potatoes on the wire rack in a single layer, shut the door of the air fryer oven, press the time button, press the +/- button to adjust the cooking time to 15 minutes, and let it cook until crisp, turning halfway.
8. Serve straight away.

Nutrition Value:

- Calories: 205 Cal
- Fat: 7 g
- Carbs: 32 g
- Protein: 4 g
- Fiber: 3 g

Veggie Fries Medley

Preparation time: 10 minutes
Cooking time: 30 minutes
Servings: 4

Ingredients:

- 2 large sweet potatoes, peeled, cut into ½-inch sticks
- 1 teaspoon garlic powder
- 4 large parsnips, peeled, cut into ½-inch sticks
- 1 teaspoon salt
- 4 carrots, cut into ½-inch sticks
- 2 tablespoons chopped rosemary
- 2 tablespoons olive oil

Method:

1. Plugin the GoWise Air Fryer Oven, turn it on, insert the parchment lined wire rack, and then press the menu button to select "vegetables"; make sure the door of the oven is closed.
2. Press the temp button, and then press the +/- button to adjust the temperature to 350 degrees F, press the time button, and then press the +/- button to adjust the cooking time to 5 minutes and let the air fryer oven preheat.
3. Meanwhile, take three separate shallow dishes, place sweet potato sticks, parsnip sticks, and carrot sticks into each dish, drizzle with oil, season with salt and black pepper and then toss until coated.
4. Spread sweet potato sticks on the wire rack in a single layer, press the time button, press the +/- button to adjust the cooking time to 10 minutes, and let it cook until crisp.
5. Then spread parsnip sticks on the wire rack in the single layer, press the time button, press the +/- button to adjust the cooking time to 4 minutes, and let it cook until crisp.
6. Then spread carrot sticks on the wire rack in a single layer, press the time button, press the +/- button to adjust the cooking time to 15 minutes, and let it cook until crisp.
7. Serve straight away.

Nutrition Value:

- Calories: 110 Cal
- Fat: 4.7 g
- Carbs: 17.4 g
- Protein: 1.5 g
- Fiber: 4 g

Chapter 8: Snacks

Pop-Tarts

Preparation time: 15 minutes
Cooking time: 30 minutes
Servings: 4

Ingredients:

For the Pop-tarts:

- 1 banana, sliced
- 2 cups self-rising flour
- 4 tablespoons strawberry jam
- 2 cups Greek yogurt
- 4 tablespoons Nutella

For the Glaze:

- Red food coloring as needed
- ¼ cup powdered sugar, divided
- 1 teaspoon vanilla extract, unsweetened
- 1 tablespoon cream
- Rainbow sprinkles as needed

Method:

1. Prepare the dough and for this, take a large bowl, place flour in it, add yogurt and then stir well until the dough comes together.
2. Transfer the dough onto a clean working space dusted with flour, knead it for 5 minutes, roll the dough, and then cut out sixteen rectangles from it.
3. Spoon 1 tablespoon of strawberry jam on top of four rectangles, cover with four rectangles and then seal them by pinching their sides with a fork.
4. Spoon 1 tablespoon of Nutella on top of four rectangles, top with a banana slice, cover with remaining four rectangles and then seal them by pinching their sides with a fork.
5. Plugin the GoWise Air Fryer Oven, turn it on, insert the parchment-lined wire rack, and then press the menu button to select "manual"; make sure the door of the oven is closed.
6. Press the temp button, and then press the +/- button to adjust the temperature to 400 degrees F, press the time button, and then press the +/- button to adjust the cooking time to 5 minutes and let the air fryer oven preheat.

7. Arrange the prepared pop tarts on the wire rack in the single layer, press the time button, press the +/- button to adjust the cooking time to 10 minutes, and let it cook until done, flipping halfway.
8. Meanwhile, prepare the glaze and for this, take a small bowl, place ¼ cup powdered sugar in it, add vanilla, cream, and food color and then whisk until combined.
9. When pop tarts have cooked, drizzle the prepared glaze over the tarts and then let them rest until the glaze turns hard.
10. Serve straight away.

Nutrition Value:

- Calories: 190 Cal
- Fat: 4.5 g
- Carbs: 35 g
- Protein: 2 g
- Fiber: 0.5 g

Fried Oreos

Preparation time: 10 minutes
Cooking time: 4 minutes
Servings: 9

Ingredients:

- 1 crescent sheet roll
- 9 Oreo cookies
- 1 teaspoon ground cinnamon
- 1 tablespoon powdered sugar

Method:

1. Plugin the GoWise Air Fryer Oven, turn it on, insert the parchment-lined wire rack, and then press the menu button to select "manual"; make sure the door of the oven is closed.
2. Press the temp button, press the +/- button to adjust the temperature to 360 degrees F, press the time button, and then press the +/- button to adjust the cooking time to 5 minutes and let the air fryer oven preheat.
3. Meanwhile, take out the crescent sheet roll, cut it into nine evenly size squares, and then roll each square on the cookie.
4. Arranged prepared cookies on the wire rack, press the time button, press the +/- button to adjust the cooking time to 4 minutes, and let it cook until done, turning halfway.
5. Sprinkle powdered sugar and cinnamon on the cookies and then serve.

Nutrition Value:

- Calories: 67 Cal
- Fat: 3 g
- Carbs: 10 g
- Protein: 1 g
- Fiber: 1 g

Spicy Peanuts

Preparation time: 10 minutes
Cooking time: 18 minutes
Servings: 4

Ingredients:

- 1 ½ cups peanuts
- 1 tablespoon cayenne pepper
- ¼ cup of sugar
- 1 tablespoon butter, unsalted
- 1/8 cup water

Method:

1. Take a large bowl, place peanuts in it, add cayenne pepper and sugar, and then stir until well mixed.
2. Plugin the GoWise Air Fryer Oven, turn it on, insert the parchment-lined wire rack, and then press the menu button to select "manual"; make sure the door of the oven is closed.
3. Press the temp button, press the +/- button to adjust the temperature to 300 degrees F, press the time button, and then press the +/- button to adjust the cooking time to 5 minutes and let the air fryer oven preheat.
4. Meanwhile, take a heatproof bowl, place butter in it, add water and then microwave for 1 minute until butter melts; stir until combined.
5. Add butter mixture into the peanuts, toss until coated, and then spread on the wire rack.
6. Press the time button, press the +/- button to adjust the cooking time to 18 minutes and let it cook until done, stirring halfway.
7. Serve straight away.

Nutrition Value:

- Calories: 244 Cal
- Fat: 18 g
- Carbs: 15 g
- Protein: 9.5 g
- Fiber: 3.3 g

Roasted Tomatillo Salsa

Preparation time: 20 minutes
Cooking time: 10 minutes
Servings: 16

Ingredients:

- ¼ of a medium white onion, peeled, chopped
- 6 tomatillos, halved
- ½ cup cilantro
- 2 cloves of garlic, peeled
- 1 jalapeno pepper, halved
- ½ teaspoon salt
- 1 lime, juiced
- 2 tablespoons olive oil

Method:

1. Plugin the GoWise Air Fryer Oven, turn it on, insert the parchment lined wire rack, and then press the menu button to select "manual"; make sure the door of the oven is closed.
2. Press the temp button, and then press the +/- button to adjust the temperature to 400 degrees F, press the time button, and then press the +/- button to adjust the cooking time to 5 minutes and let the air fryer oven preheat.
3. Meanwhile, take a large bowl, place tomatillo and jalapeno pepper pieces in it, drizzle with oil, season with ¼ teaspoon salt and then toss until coated.
4. Spread the vegetables on the wire rack in the single layer, press the time button, press the +/- button to adjust the cooking time to 10 minutes, and let it cook, tossing halfway.
5. Let the vegetables cool for 10 minutes, transfer them into a food processor, add remaining ingredients, and then pulse until smooth.
6. Serve straight away.

Nutrition Value:

- Calories: 9.9 Cal
- Fat: 1 g
- Carbs: 2 g
- Protein: 0 g
- Fiber: 1 g

Cheeseburger Tater Tot Bites

Preparation time: 10 minutes
Cooking time: 18 minutes
Servings: 8

Ingredients:

- 1 pound ground beef
- 2 tablespoons dill pickle relish
- ½ of a medium white onion, peeled, diced
- 1 teaspoon salt
- 2 tablespoons yellow mustard
- ½ teaspoon ground black pepper
- 2 tablespoons mayonnaise
- 2 tablespoons ketchup
- 1 cup shredded cheddar cheese
- 63 frozen tater tots

Method:

1. Plugin the GoWise Air Fryer Oven, turn it on, insert the wire rack, and then press the menu button to select "manual"; make sure the door of the oven is closed.
2. Press the temp button, and then press the +/- button to adjust the temperature to 350 degrees F, press the time button, and then press the +/- button to adjust the cooking time to 5 minutes and let the air fryer oven preheat.
3. Meanwhile, take 21 muffin cups and then place three frozen tater tots into each cup.
4. Arrange the muffin cups on the wire rack, press the time button, press the +/- button to adjust the cooking time to 7 minutes, and let it cook.
5. Meanwhile, take a medium skillet pan, place it over medium-high heat, and let it heat until hot.
6. Add beef, cook for 5 minutes until golden brown, then drain the grease and stir in onion.
7. Cook beef and onion for 2 to 3 minutes until the onion turns soft, and then remove the pan from heat.
8. Add relish, ketchup, mustard, and mayonnaise, stir until combined, and then season the beef mixture with salt and black pepper.
9. When tater tots have cooked, top them evenly with beef mixture, sprinkle with cheese, return muffin cups into the air fryer oven and then continue cooking for 10 minutes.
10. Serve straight away.

Nutrition Value:

- Calories: 106.3 Cal
- Fat: 7 g
- Carbs: 5.2 g

- Protein: 5 g
- Fiber: 0.2 g

Beef Jerky

Preparation time: 40 minutes
Cooking time: 6 hours
Servings: 16

Ingredients:

- 2 pounds flank steak, frozen
- 1 teaspoon onion powder
- ½ teaspoon garlic powder
- 1 teaspoon seasoned salt
- 2 teaspoons ground black pepper
- 2 tablespoons Worcestershire sauce
- 1 teaspoon liquid smoke
- ½ cup of soy sauce

Method:

1. Cut the frozen steak into 1/8-inch thick strips and then place them in a large plastic bag
2. Take a small bowl, place the remaining ingredients, whisk until combined, and then pour it into the plastic bag
3. Seal the bag
4. turn it upside down until coated, and then let the steak strips marinate for 30 minutes.
5. Then Plugin the GoWise Air Fryer Oven, turn it on, insert the drip pan with a wire rack, and then press the menu button to select "dehydrate"; make sure the door of the oven is closed.
6. Arrange marinated steak strips on the wire rack in the single layer, press the time button, press the +/- button to adjust the time to 6 hours, and let it cook.
7. Serve straight away.

Nutrition Value:

- Calories: 42 Cal
- Fat: 0.5 g
- Carbs: 0.8 g
- Protein: 8.7 g
- Fiber: 0 g

Nana's Macaroni

Preparation time: 10 minutes
Cooking time: 30 minutes
Servings: 4

Ingredients:

- ¾ pound macaroni elbows, cooked
- 1 teaspoon salt
- ½ teaspoon ground black pepper
- ¾ stick of butter, cut into chunks
- 12 ounces tomato sauce
- 1 cup milk
- 6 ounces Colby cheese, grated

Method:

1. Plugin the GoWise Air Fryer Oven, turn it on, insert the wire rack, and then press the menu button to select "manual"; make sure the door of the oven is closed.
2. Press the temp button, and then press the +/- button to adjust the temperature to 350 degrees F, press the time button, and then press the +/- button to adjust the cooking time to 5 minutes and let the air fryer oven preheat.
3. Meanwhile, take a heatproof dish, place cooked pasta in it, and then sprinkle half of the cheese on top.
4. Pour in milk and tomato sauce, scatter butter chunks on top, sprinkle with salt and black pepper, add remaining cheese and then stir until mixed.
5. Place the prepared dish on the wire rack, press the time button, press the +/- button to adjust the cooking time to 30 minutes and let it cook.
6. Serve straight away.

Nutrition Value:

- Calories: 215.7 Cal
- Fat: 11.3 g
- Carbs: 21.4 g
- Protein: 8 g
- Fiber: 2 g

Tortilla Chips

Preparation time: 10 minutes
Cooking time: 4 minutes
Servings: 4

Ingredients:

- 4 corn tortillas
- 1 teaspoon salt
- 4 tablespoons olive oil

Method:

1. Plugin the GoWise Air Fryer Oven, turn it on, insert the wire rack, and then press the menu button to select "manual"; make sure the door of the oven is closed.
2. Press the temp button, and then press the +/- button to adjust the temperature to 350 degrees F, press the time button, and then press the +/- button to adjust the cooking time to 5 minutes and let the air fryer oven preheat.
3. Meanwhile, cut each tortilla into 8 triangles, brush them with oil and then season with salt.
4. Spread tortillas on the wire rack in the single layer, press the time button, press the +/- button to adjust the cooking time to 4 minutes, and let it cook.
5. Serve straight away.

Nutrition Value:

- Calories: 112 Cal
- Fat: 5 g
- Carbs: 16 g
- Protein: 1.7 g
- Fiber: 1.3 g

Sweet Potato Fries

Preparation time: 10 minutes
Cooking time: 20 minutes
Servings: 2

Ingredients:

- 2 large sweet potatoes
- ½ teaspoon salt
- 1 tablespoon olive oil

Method:

1. Plugin the GoWise Air Fryer Oven, turn it on, insert the wire rack, and then press the menu button to select "manual"; make sure the door of the oven is closed.
2. Press the temp button, and then press the +/- button to adjust the temperature to 400 degrees F, press the time button, and then press the +/- button to adjust the cooking time to 5 minutes and let the air fryer oven preheat.
3. Meanwhile, peel the potatoes, cut them into fries, and then place them in a large bowl.
4. Add salt and oil, toss until coated, and then spread the fries on the wire rack in a single layer.
5. Press the time button, press the +/- button to adjust the cooking time to 20 minutes and let it cook until crisp, tossing halfway.
6. Serve straight away.

Nutrition Value:

- Calories: 122.4 Cal
- Fat: 4.8 g
- Carbs: 18.7 g
- Protein: 1.8 g
- Fiber: 3 g

Pepperoni Pita Pizza

Preparation time: 10 minutes
Cooking time: 8 minutes
Servings: 1

Ingredients:

- ¼ cup pepperoni slices
- 1 pita bread
- 1 teaspoon olive oil
- 2 tablespoons pizza sauce
- ¼ cup shredded mozzarella cheese

Method:

1. Plugin the GoWise Air Fryer Oven, turn it on, insert the wire rack, and then press the menu button to select "pizza"; make sure the door of the oven is closed.
2. Press the temp button, and then press the +/- button to adjust the temperature to 350 degrees F, press the time button, and then press the +/- button to adjust the cooking time to 5 minutes and let the air fryer oven preheat.
3. Meanwhile, take a small bowl, place sauce in it, and then stir in olive oil.
4. Spread the pizza sauce mixture on the pita bread, scatter pepperoni on top and then sprinkle with cheese.
5. Place the pizza on the wire rack, press the time button, press the +/- button to adjust the cooking time to 8 minutes and let it cook until done.
6. Serve straight away.

Nutrition Value:

- Calories: 296.2 Cal
- Fat: 10.7 g
- Carbs: 33.7 g
- Protein: 18.7 g
- Fiber: 1.5 g

Mac and Cheese Balls

Preparation time: 10 minutes
Cooking time: 10 minutes
Servings: 4

Ingredients:

- 4 cups cooked mac and cheese
- 1 tablespoon milk
- 4 tablespoons olive oil
- 1 ½ cups seasoned breadcrumbs
- 1 egg

Method:

1. Plugin the GoWise Air Fryer Oven, turn it on, insert the parchment lined wire rack, and then press the menu button to select "manual"; make sure the door of the oven is closed.
2. Press the temp button, and then press the +/- button to adjust the temperature to 370 degrees F, press the time button, and then press the +/- button to adjust the cooking time to 5 minutes and let the air fryer oven preheat.
3. Meanwhile, take a medium bowl, crack the egg in it, pour in the milk and then whisk well until blended.
4. Take a shallow dish and then place breadcrumbs in it.
5. Cut the cooked mac and cheese into balls.
6. Working on one ball at a time, each ball into the egg
7. dredge into the breadcrumbs until coated, and then coat with oil.
8. Arrange the mac and cheese balls on the wire rack, press the time button, press the +/- button to adjust the cooking time to 10 minutes and let it cook until done, turning halfway.
9. Serve straight away.

Nutrition Value:

- Calories: 220.7 Cal
- Fat: 8.9 g
- Carbs: 24.5 g
- Protein: 10.8 g
- Fiber: 1.2 g

Apple Chips

Preparation time: 10 minutes
Cooking time: 1 hour
Servings: 1

Ingredients:

- 1 large red apple, cored, thinly sliced
- 1 teaspoon cinnamon powder
- 1 tablespoon brown sugar
- 2 tablespoons sugar

Method:

1. Plugin the GoWise Air Fryer Oven, turn it on, insert the wire rack, and then press the menu button to select "manual"; make sure the door of the oven is closed.
2. Press the temp button, and then press the +/- button to adjust the temperature to 250 degrees F, press the time button, and then press the +/- button to adjust the cooking time to 5 minutes and let the air fryer oven preheat.
3. Meanwhile, take a large bowl, place apple slices in it, add cinnamon and both sugar and then toss until coated.
4. Spread the apple chips on the wire rack in the single layer, press the time button, press the +/- button to adjust the cooking time to 1 hour, and let it cook until crisp.
5. When done, let the apple chips cool completely and then serve.

Nutrition Value:

- Calories: 140 Cal
- Fat: 7 g
- Carbs: 20 g
- Protein: 0 g
- Fiber: 2 g

Onion Rings

Preparation time: 15 minutes
Cooking time: 30 minutes
Servings: 2

Ingredients:

- 2 large sweet onions
- ¾ cup all-purpose flour
- ½ teaspoon onion powder
- 1 teaspoon smoked paprika
- ½ teaspoon garlic powder
- 2 teaspoons salt
- 2 cups panko breadcrumbs
- 2 eggs
- 2 tablespoons milk

Method:

1. Cut the end off from each onion, peel the skin, cut into thick slices, and then separate the rings.
2. Take a small bowl, place all the spices in it and then stir until mixed.
3. Take a shallow dish and then place flour in it and then stir in one-third of the spice mixture.
4. Take another shallow dish, crack eggs in it, pour in the milk, add half of the spice mixture and then whisk until combined.
5. Take another shallow dish, place breadcrumbs in it, and then stir in the remaining spice mixture.
6. Plugin the GoWise Air Fryer Oven, turn it on, insert the parchment-lined wire rack, and then press the menu button to select "manual"; make sure the door of the oven is closed.
7. Press the temp button, and then press the +/- button to adjust the temperature to 375 degrees F, press the time button, and then press the +/- button to adjust the cooking time to 5 minutes and let the air fryer oven preheat.
8. Meanwhile, working on one onion ring at a time, dredge in flour, dip into the egg and then dredge into the breadcrumbs until coated.
9. Arrange the prepared onion rings on the wire rack, spray with oil, press the time button, press the +/- button to adjust the cooking time to 10 minutes, and let it cook until golden brown, turning halfway.
10. Serve straight away.

Nutrition Value:

- Calories: 196 Cal
- Fat: 2 g
- Carbs: 36 g
- Protein: 8 g
- Fiber: 2 g

Sweet and Spicy Nuts

Preparation time: 10 minutes
Cooking time: 12 minutes
Servings: 3

Ingredients:

- 1 ½ cups peanuts
- 1 tablespoon cayenne pepper
- ¼ cup sugar
- 2 tablespoons water
- 1 tablespoon butter, unsalted

Method:

1. Plugin the GoWise Air Fryer Oven, turn it on, insert the parchment-lined wire rack, and then press the menu button to select "manual"; make sure the door of the oven is closed.
2. Press the temp button, press the +/- button to adjust the temperature to 300 degrees F, press the time button, and then press the +/- button to adjust the cooking time to 5 minutes and let the air fryer oven preheat.
3. Meanwhile, take a large bowl, place peanuts in it and then stir in cayenne pepper and sugar until combined.
4. Take a small heatproof bowl, place butter in it, add water, microwave for 1 minute until butter melts; stir until combined.
5. Drizzle the butter mixture over peanuts, toss until mixed, and then spread on the wire rack.
6. Press the time button, press the +/- button to adjust the cooking time to 12 minutes and let it cook until done, turning halfway.
7. Serve straight away.

Nutrition Value:

- Calories: 241.6 Cal
- Fat: 18 g
- Carbs: 16.2 g
- Protein: 7.6 g
- Fiber: 4.3 g

Hawaiian Tortilla Pizza

Preparation time: 10 minutes
Cooking time: 8 minutes
Servings: 1

Ingredients:

- 1 flour tortilla
- 1 hot dog
- sliced
- ¼ cup pineapple cubes
- 1 slice of ham, cubed
- 2 tablespoons tomato sauce
- ¼ cup shredded mozzarella cheese

Method:

1. Plugin the GoWise Air Fryer Oven, turn it on, insert the wire rack, and then press the menu button to select "pizza"; make sure the door of the oven is closed.
2. Press the temp button, and then press the +/- button to adjust the temperature to 350 degrees F, press the time button, and then press the +/- button to adjust the cooking time to 5 minutes and let the air fryer oven preheat.
3. Meanwhile, spread tomato sauce on the tortilla, scatter pineapple, hot dog
4. and ham pieces on top, and then sprinkle with cheese.
5. Place the pizza on the wire rack, press the time button, press the +/- button to adjust the cooking time to 8 minutes, and let it cook until done.
6. Serve straight away.

Nutrition Value:

- Calories: 329.7 Cal
- Fat: 11.3 g
- Carbs: 38.8 g
- Protein: 21 g
- Fiber: 5.6 g

Popcorn

Preparation time: 10 minutes
Cooking time: 7 minutes
Servings: 2

Ingredients:

- ½ cup of corn
- 1 teaspoon brown sugar
- ½ teaspoon olive oil
- 1 tablespoon melted butter

Method:

1. Plugin the GoWise Air Fryer Oven, turn it on, insert the mesh basket, and then press the menu button to select "manual"; make sure the door of the oven is closed.
2. Press the temp button, and then press the +/- button to adjust the temperature to 400 degrees F, press the time button, and then press the +/- button to adjust the cooking time to 5 minutes and let the air fryer oven preheat.
3. Meanwhile, take a medium bowl, place corn in it, add oil, and then toss until coated.
4. Spread the corns in the mesh basket in the single layer, press the time button, press the +/- button to adjust the cooking time to 7 minutes, and let it cook until all the corns have popped.
5. When done, drizzle melted butter over the popcorns, sprinkle with sugar and then serve.

Nutrition Value:

- Calories: 77 Cal
- Fat: 7 g
- Carbs: 4 g
- Protein: 1 g
- Fiber: 1 g

Croutons

Preparation time: 10 minutes
Cooking time: 13 minutes
Servings: 6

Ingredients:

- 6 slices of Texas toast, cubed
- ½ tablespoon salt
- 1 teaspoon red chili powder
- ½ tablespoon ground black pepper
- ¼ cup olive oil

Method:

1. Plugin the GoWise Air Fryer Oven, turn it on, insert the mesh rack, and then press the menu button to select "manual"; make sure the door of the oven is closed.
2. Press the temp button, and then press the +/- button to adjust the temperature to 250 degrees F, press the time button, and then press the +/- button to adjust the cooking time to 5 minutes and let the air fryer oven preheat.
3. Meanwhile, take a large bowl, place toast cubes in it, add remaining ingredients and then toss until well coated.
4. Spread the toast pieces on the mesh rack in a single layer, press the time button, press the +/- button to adjust the cooking time to 13 minutes, and let it cook until crisp.
5. Serve straight away.

Nutrition Value:

- Calories: 80 Cal
- Fat: 2.2 g
- Carbs: 13 g
- Protein: 2 g
- Fiber: 0.7 g

Pepperoni Chips

Preparation time: 10 minutes
Cooking time: 16 minutes
Servings: 2

Ingredients:

- 30 slices of pepperoni

Method:

1. Plugin the GoWise Air Fryer Oven, turn it on, insert the wire rack, and then press the menu button to select "manual"; make sure the door of the oven is closed.
2. Press the temp button, and then press the +/- button to adjust the temperature to 360 degrees F, press the time button, and then press the +/- button to adjust the cooking time to 5 minutes and let the air fryer oven preheat.
3. Meanwhile, spread the pepperoni slices on the wire rack in a single layer, press the time button, press the +/- button to adjust the cooking time to 8 minutes, and let it cook.
4. Serve straight away.

Nutrition Value:

- Calories: 148 Cal
- Fat: 13 g
- Carbs: 2 g
- Protein: 7 g
- Fiber: 1 g

Mozzarella Sticks

Preparation time: 10 minutes
Cooking time: 10 minutes
Servings: 2

Ingredients:

- 12 sticks of mozzarella cheese, about 1-ounce, frozen
- ¼ cup all-purpose flour
- ¼ teaspoon salt
- 1 ½ tablespoon Italian seasoning
- ¼ teaspoon ground black pepper
- 1 ½ cup panko breadcrumbs
- 1 egg

Method:

1. Take a shallow dish, place breadcrumbs in it, add salt, black pepper, Italian seasoning in it and then stir until mixed.
2. Take a separate shallow dish, crack the egg in it and then whisk until combined.
3. Take another separate dish and then place flour in it.
4. Working on one cheese stick at a time, dredge in flour, dip into the egg
5. dredge in breadcrumbs until coated, and then freeze for 15 minutes.
6. Meanwhile, Plugin the GoWise Air Fryer Oven, turn it on, insert the parchment-lined wire rack, and then press the menu button to select "manual"; make sure the door of the oven is closed.
7. Press the temp button, press the +/- button to adjust the temperature to 350 degrees F, press the time button, and then press the +/- button to adjust the cooking time to 5 minutes and let the air fryer oven preheat.
8. Arrange the cheese sticks on the wire rack, press the time button, press the +/- button to adjust the cooking time to 10 minutes, and let it cook until golden brown, flipping halfway.
9. Serve straight away.

Nutrition Value:

- Calories: 164.3 Cal
- Fat: 6.2 g
- Carbs: 8 g
- Protein: 14 g
- Fiber: 0 g

Zucchini Chips

Preparation time: 10 minutes
Cooking time: 8 minutes
Servings: 4

Ingredients:

- 2 large zucchini, cut into slices
- ¼ cup all-purpose flour
- ½ cup panko breadcrumbs
- 2 eggs

Method:

1. Plugin the GoWise Air Fryer Oven, turn it on, insert the parchment-lined wire rack, and then press the menu button to select "manual"; make sure the door of the oven is closed.
2. Press the temp button, and then press the +/- button to adjust the temperature to 355 degrees F, press the time button, and then press the +/- button to adjust the cooking time to 5 minutes and let the air fryer oven preheat.
3. Meanwhile, take three shallow dishes and then place flour, whisked egg
4. and breadcrumbs into each dish.
5. Working on one zucchini slice at a time, dredge in flour, dip in egg and then dredge in breadcrumbs until coated.
6. Arrange the zucchini chips on the wire rack in the single layer, press the time button, press the +/- button to adjust the cooking time to 8 minutes and let it cook until done, flipping halfway.
7. Serve straight away.

Nutrition Value:

- Calories: 60.8 Cal
- Fat: 0.4 g
- Carbs: 14.4 g
- Protein: 2.4 g
- Fiber: 5.2 g

BBQ Chickpeas

Preparation time: 10 minutes
Cooking time: 22 minutes
Servings: 3

Ingredients:

- 2 cups cooked chickpeas

For the Seasoning:

- ½ teaspoon mustard powder
- 1 teaspoon brown sugar
- ½ teaspoon celery salt
- ¼ teaspoon ground black pepper
- ½ teaspoon garlic powder
- 1 ½ teaspoon paprika

Method:

1. Plugin the GoWise Air Fryer Oven, turn it on, insert the mesh basket and then press the menu button to select "manual"; make sure the door of the oven is closed.
2. Press the temp button, and then press the +/- button to adjust the temperature to 390 degrees F, press the time button, and then press the +/- button to adjust the cooking time to 5 minutes and let the air fryer oven preheat.
3. Meanwhile, take a small bowl, place all the ingredients for the seasoning in it and then stir until mixed.
4. Spread chickpeas on the mesh basket, press the time button, press the +/- button to adjust the cooking time to 5 minutes, and let it cook.
5. Then spray oil over the chickpeas and continue air frying for 10 minutes, stirring halfway.
6. Sprinkle half of the seasoning on the chickpeas and then continue air frying for 2 minutes.
7. When done, transfer chickpeas to a bowl, add remaining seasoning
8. and then toss until coated.
9. Serve straight away.

Nutrition Value:

- Calories: 121 Cal
- Fat: 4 g
- Carbs: 16 g
- Protein: 6 g
- Fiber: 5 g

Chapter 9: Desserts

Pistachio Cookies

Preparation time: 1 hour and 10 minutes
Cooking time: 12 minutes
Servings: 6

Ingredients:

- ¾ cups all-purpose flour
- ½ package of instant pudding mix, pistachio flavor
- 1 teaspoon vanilla extract, unsweetened
- ¼ cup powdered sugar and more as needed
- 1 stick of butter, salted, softened

Method:

1. Take a large bowl, place butter in it, and then whisk until smooth.
2. Beat in sugar until fluffy and then beat in vanilla until combined.
3. Take a separate large bowl, place flour in it, add pudding mix, stir until combined, and then stir into the butter mixture until dough comes together.
4. Wrap the bowl with a plastic wrap, place it into the refrigerator, and then let it rest for 1 hour.
5. Then Plugin the GoWise Air Fryer Oven, turn it on, insert the parchment-lined wire rack, and then press the menu button to select "manual"; make sure the door of the oven is closed.
6. Press the temp button, press the +/- button to adjust the temperature to 350 degrees F, press the time button, and then press the +/- button to adjust the cooking time to 5 minutes and let the air fryer oven preheat.
7. Meanwhile, remove dough from the refrigerator and then shape it into cookie balls, each about 1 tablespoon of dough and then roll each ball into powdered sugar.
8. Arrange the cookie ball on the parchment-lined wire rack, press the time button, press the +/- button to adjust the cooking time to 6 minutes, and let it cook until done.
9. When done, sprinkle some more sugar on cookies and then serve.

Nutrition Value:

- Calories: 147.4 Cal
- Fat: 6 g
- Carbs: 21.6 g
- Protein: 3 g

- Fiber: 1.2 g

Apple Cider Snickerdoodles

Preparation time: 2 hours and 10 minutes
Cooking time: 8 minutes
Servings: 6

Ingredients:

- 2 cups all-purpose flour
- ½ teaspoon ground cinnamon
- ¼ teaspoon salt
- ½ cup sugar
- ¼ teaspoon ground cloves
- 1/3 cup brown sugar
- ½ cup butter, unsalted, softened

- 1 teaspoon cream of tartar
- ½ teaspoon vanilla extract, unsweetened
- 1 egg
- ½ teaspoon baking soda
- 1/3 cup apple cider

For Rolling:

- 1 teaspoon ground cinnamon
- ¼ cup of sugar

Method:

1. Take a large bowl, place flour in it, add salt, cloves, cinnamon, and baking soda and then stir until mixed.
2. Take a separate large bowl, place butter in it, beat until creamy and then beat in both sugars until smooth.
3. Beat in egg
4. vanilla, and apple cider until combined, and then beat in flour mixture until incorporated and dough comes together.
5. Wrap the bowl tightly with a plastic wrap and then place it in the refrigerator for 2 hours.
6. Then Plugin the GoWise Air Fryer Oven, turn it on, insert the parchment-lined mesh rack, and then press the menu button to select "manual"; make sure the door of the oven is closed.
7. Take a small bowl, place sugar and cinnamon, and then stir until mixed.
8. Press the temp button, and then press the +/- button to adjust the temperature to 350 degrees F, press the time button, and then press the +/- button to adjust the cooking time to 5 minutes and let the air fryer oven preheat.
9. Meanwhile, remove the dough from the refrigerator, shape it into 1-inch balls, and then roll into the sugar-cinnamon mixture.

10. Arrange the balls on the mesh rack, press the time button, press the +/- button to adjust the cooking time to 8 minutes and let it cook until done.
11. Serve straight away.

Nutrition Value:

- Calories: 240 Cal
- Fat: 12 g
- Carbs: 32 g
- Protein: 4 g
- Fiber: 1 g

Avocado Brownies

Preparation time: 10 minutes
Cooking time: 15 minutes
Servings: 2

Ingredients:

- 2 avocados, peeled, pitted
- 2/3 cup cocoa powder, unsweetened
- 2/3 cup sugar
- 6 tablespoons peanut butter
- 4 eggs
- 2 teaspoons baking soda
- 2 teaspoons vanilla extract, unsweetened
- ½ cup coconut oil

Method:

1. Plugin the GoWise Air Fryer Oven, turn it on, insert the wire rack, and then press the menu button to select "manual"; make sure the door of the oven is closed.
2. Press the temp button, and then press the +/- button to adjust the temperature to 350 degrees F, press the time button, and then press the +/- button to adjust the cooking time to 5 minutes and let the air fryer oven preheat.
3. Meanwhile, place all the ingredients in a food processor, pulse until smooth batter comes together, and then spoon into a 9-inch springform pan.
4. Press the time button, press the +/- button to adjust the cooking time to 15 minutes and let it cook until done.
5. When done, let the brownies cool completely, cut into squares, and then serve.

Nutrition Value:

- Calories: 139 Cal
- Fat: 8.3 g
- Carbs: 15.7 g
- Protein: 3 g
- Fiber: 4 g

Cardamom Crinkles

Preparation time: 20 minutes
Cooking time: 12 minutes
Servings: 6

Ingredients:

- 2¼ cups all-purpose flour
- ¾ teaspoon ground cardamom
- ½ teaspoon ground cinnamon
- 1 cup brown sugar

- ¼ cup molasses
- ¾ cup shortening
- 1 teaspoon baking soda
- 1 egg

For the Coating:

- ¼ cup sugar

- ½ teaspoon ground cinnamon

Method:

1. Plugin the GoWise Air Fryer Oven, turn it on, insert the parchment-lined wire rack, and then press the menu button to select "bake"; make sure the door of the oven is closed.
2. Press the temp button, and then press the +/- button to adjust the temperature to 375 degrees F, press the time button, and then press the +/- button to adjust the cooking time to 5 minutes and let the air fryer oven preheat.
3. Meanwhile, take a large bowl, place shortening in it, and then beat until creamy.
4. Beat in cinnamon, cardamom, baking soda, and sugar until well combined, beat in egg and molasses until mixed and then beat in flour until incorporated.
5. Take a small bowl, place sugar and cinnamon in it, and then stir until mixed.
6. Shape the dough into 1 ½ inches balls, roll them into the sugar-cinnamon mixture and then arrange them on the wire rack.
7. Press the time button, press the +/- button to adjust the cooking time to 12 minutes, and let it cook until done.
8. Serve straight away.

Nutrition Value:

- Calories: 163 Cal
- Fat: 6 g
- Carbs: 26 g

- Protein: 2 g
- Fiber: 1 g

Pumpkin Cake

Preparation time: 10 minutes
Cooking time: 40 minutes
Servings: 4

Ingredients:

- 18 ounces yellow cake mix
- 15 ounces pumpkin
- 1 ½ cups chopped walnuts
- 1 cup of sugar
- 12 ounces evaporated milk
- 4 teaspoons pumpkin pie spice
- ¾ cup butter, unsalted, melted
- 3 eggs

Method:

1. Plugin the GoWise Air Fryer Oven, turn it on, insert the wire rack, and then press the menu button to select "manual"; make sure the door of the oven is closed.
2. Press the temp button, press the +/- button to adjust the temperature to 350 degrees F, press the time button, and then press the +/- button to adjust the cooking time to 5 minutes and let the air fryer oven preheat.
3. Meanwhile, take a large bowl, place the pumpkin in it, add sugar, pumpkin pie spice, and eggs, pour in the milk, and then whisk until smooth.
4. Take a heatproof baking dish, grease it with oil, spoon half of the pumpkin mixture in it and then sprinkle half of the cake mix on top.
5. Drizzle half of the butter on top of the cake mix, scatter ¾ cup walnuts on top and then repeat by using the remaining pumpkin mixture, cake mix, butter, and walnuts.
6. Place the baking dish on the wire rack, press the time button, press the +/- button to adjust the cooking time to 40 minutes, and let it cook until done.
7. Let the cake cool completely, cut it into slices, and then serve.

Nutrition Value:

- Calories: 270.9 Cal
- Fat: 12.5 g
- Carbs: 36.6 g
- Protein: 4.6 g
- Fiber: 2.4 g

Fried Banana Smores

Preparation time: 10 minutes
Cooking time: 6 minutes
Servings: 4

Ingredients:

- 4 bananas
- 4 tablespoons peanut butter chips
- 4 tablespoons graham cracker cereal
- 4 tablespoons marshmallows
- 4 tablespoons mini chocolate chips, semi-sweet

Method:

1. Plugin the GoWise Air Fryer Oven, turn it on, insert the parchment lined wire rack, and then press the menu button to select "manual"; make sure the door of the oven is closed.
2. Press the temp button, and then press the +/- button to adjust the temperature to 400 degrees F, press the time button, and then press the +/- button to adjust the cooking time to 5 minutes and let the air fryer oven preheat.
3. Meanwhile, slice the banana lengthwise and then open it slightly to form a pocket.
4. Fill each pocket of banana with marshmallows, peanut butter chips, and chocolate chips, and then stuff with the cereal.
5. Arrange the bananas on the wire rack, press the time button, press the +/- button to adjust the cooking time to 6 minutes and let it cook until marshmallow have toasted and bananas turn soft.
6. Serve straight away.

Nutrition Value:

- Calories: 264.4 Cal
- Fat: 12.1 g
- Carbs: 34 g
- Protein: 1.3 g
- Fiber: 2.8 g

Slime-Filled Cookies

Preparation time: 15 minutes
Cooking time: 15 minutes
Servings: 6

Ingredients:

- 2 ½ cups all-purpose flour
- 1 cup brown sugar
- 1 cup of cocoa powder
- 2 teaspoons vanilla extract, unsweetened
- 1 cup white sugar
- ¼ cup baking powder
- 2 eggs
- 1 ½ cups butter, salted, softened
- 32 green gummy candies
- Black food coloring as needed

Method:

1. Take a large bowl, place butter in it, add white and brown sugar in it, beat until creamy and then beat in vanilla and eggs until combined.
2. Beat in baking powder, cocoa powder, and flour until incorporated and then shape the dough into dough balls, each ball about 2 tablespoons of dough.
3. Break each ball in half, place a candy, and then seal it with the dough.
4. Plugin the GoWise Air Fryer Oven, turn it on, insert the parchment-lined wire rack, and then press the menu button to select "manual"; make sure the door of the oven is closed.
5. Press the temp button, press the +/- button to adjust the temperature to 350 degrees F, press the time button, and then press the +/- button to adjust the cooking time to 5 minutes and let the air fryer oven preheat.
6. Arrange the balls on the wire rack, press the time button, press the +/- button to adjust the cooking time to 5 minutes, and let it cook.
7. Serve straight away.

Nutrition Value:

- Calories: 220 Cal
- Fat: 8 g
- Carbs: 35 g
- Protein: 2 g
- Fiber: 0.5 g

Brownie Cheesecake

Preparation time: 15 minutes
Cooking time: 20 minutes
Servings: 2

Ingredients:

For the Brownie Layer:

- ½ cup all-purpose flour
- ½ cup of cocoa powder
- 1 cup of sugar
- ½ teaspoon salt
- ¼ teaspoon baking powder
- 1 teaspoon vanilla extract, unsweetened
- ½ cup olive oil
- 2 eggs

For the Cheesecake Layer:

- 10 drops of yellow food coloring
- ¼ cup of sugar
- 8 ounces cream cheese, softened
- 10 drops of red food coloring
- 1 egg

Method:

1. Plugin the GoWise Air Fryer Oven, turn it on, insert the mesh rack, and then press the menu button to select "manual"; make sure the door of the oven is closed.
2. Press the temp button, and then press the +/- button to adjust the temperature to 350 degrees F, press the time button, and then press the +/- button to adjust the cooking time to 5 minutes and let the air fryer oven preheat.
3. Meanwhile, prepare the brownie layer and for this, take a large bowl, place all of its ingredients in it and then whisk until combined and smooth batter comes together.
4. Take an 8-inch pan and then spoon the prepared brownie batter in it, reserving ¼ cup of the batter.
5. Prepare the cheesecake layer and for this, take a medium bowl, place all of its ingredients in it and then whisk until smooth.
6. Spread the batter for the cheesecake layer on top of the brownie layer, top with reserved batter for the brownie layer, and then swirl it using a fork or a skewer.
7. Place the pan on the wire rack, press the time button, press the +/- button to adjust the cooking time to 20 minutes, and let it cook until done.
8. When done, let the cake cool completely, cut it into slices, and then serve.

Nutrition Value:

- Calories: 410.2 Cal
- Fat: 24 g
- Carbs: 46 g

- Protein: 15 g
- Fiber: 2 g

Baked Apple

Preparation time: 10 minutes
Cooking time: 20 minutes
Servings: 2

Ingredients:

- 1 medium apple
- ¼ teaspoon ground cinnamon
- 2 tablespoons walnuts, chopped
- ¼ teaspoon ground nutmeg
- 2 tablespoons raisins
- ¼ cup of water
- 1 ½ teaspoons butter, unsalted, melted

Method:

1. Plugin the GoWise Air Fryer Oven, turn it on, insert the wire rack, and then press the menu button to select "manual"; make sure the door of the oven is closed.
2. Press the temp button, press the +/- button to adjust the temperature to 350 degrees F, press the time button, and then press the +/- button to adjust the cooking time to 5 minutes and let the air fryer oven preheat.
3. Meanwhile, take a small bowl, place walnuts and raisins in it, add cinnamon, nutmeg
4. and butter and then stir until mixed.
5. Cut the apple in half, spoon some of its flesh from the middle, and stuff with the walnut mixture.
6. Take a cake pan, pour water in it, place the stuffed apples in it and then place the pan on the wire rack.
7. Press the time button, press the +/- button to adjust the cooking time to 20 minutes, and let it cook.
8. Serve straight away.

Nutrition Value:

- Calories: 89 Cal
- Fat: 0 g
- Carbs: 23 g
- Protein: 0 g
- Fiber: 2 g

Chapter 10: 30-Day Meal Plan

Day 1

Breakfast: Apple, Pecan and Quinoa Granola

Lunch: Hawaiian Tortilla Pizza

Dinner: Breaded Whole Chicken

Dessert: Slime-Filled Cookies

Day 2

Breakfast: Avocado Egg Boat

Lunch: Bacon Wrapped Serranos

Dinner: Low Country Boil Skewers

Dessert: Brownie Cheesecake

Day 3

Breakfast: Pumpkin Spice Muffins

Lunch: Egg Rolls

Dinner: Orange Soda Chicken Wings

Dessert: Avocado Brownies

Day 4

Breakfast: Five Cheese Pull-Apart Bread

Lunch: Pork Chops

Dinner: Baby Back Ribs

Dessert: Cardamom Crinkles

Day 5

Breakfast: Strawberry Rhubarb Crumbles

Lunch: Tornado Potato

Dinner: Shrimp and Sausage Veggie Skewers

Dessert: Pistachio Cookies

Day 6

Breakfast: French Toast Sticks

Lunch: Tuna Melts

Dinner: Game Day Burgers

Dessert: Baked Apple

Day 7

Breakfast: Bacon and Egg Bites

Lunch: Roasted Rainbow Vegetables

Dinner: Pork Chops with Broccoli

Dessert: Pumpkin Cake

Day 8

Breakfast: Spiced Applesauce Bread

Lunch: Greek Chicken Kebabs

Dinner: Italian Chicken Skewers

Dessert: Fried Banana Smores

Day 9

Breakfast: Egg in a Hole

Lunch: Spring Rolls with Tofu

Dinner: Crumbed Fish

Dessert: Apple Cider Snickerdoodles

Day 10

Breakfast: Breakfast Muffins

Lunch: Salmon

Dinner: Sesame Cauliflower Wings

Dessert: Slime-Filled Cookies

Day 11

Breakfast: Sweet Potato Toast

Lunch: Bacon Wrapped Brussel Sprouts

Dinner: Cherry Glazed Chicken Wings

Dessert: Brownie Cheesecake

Day 12

Breakfast: Cranberry Muffins

Lunch: Mummy Hotdogs

Dinner: Fish Cakes

Dessert: Avocado Brownies

Day 13

Breakfast: Bread Rolls

Lunch: Breaded Pork Chops

Dinner: Korean BBQ Chicken Skewers

Dessert: Cardamom Crinkles

Day 14

Breakfast: Cheese and Vegetables Egg Cups

Lunch: Bacon Wrapped Shrimp

Dinner: Pecan Crusted Halibut

Dessert: Pistachio Cookies

Day 15

Breakfast: Jalapeno Cornbread

Lunch: Mexican Beef Kebabs

Dinner: Cauliflower Fritters

Dessert: Baked Apple

Day 16

Breakfast: Apple, Pecan and Quinoa Granola

Lunch: Garlic and Herb Pork Chops

Dinner: Vegetables, Corn and Beef Kabobs

Dessert: Pumpkin Cake

Day 17

Breakfast: Avocado Egg Boat

Lunch: Beer Battered Fish

Dinner: Pork Bites with Mushrooms

Dessert: Fried Banana Smores

Day 18

Breakfast: Pumpkin Spice Muffins

Lunch: Marinated Steaks

Dinner: Garlic Parmesan Shrimps

Dessert: Apple Cider Snickerdoodles

Day 19

Breakfast: Five Cheese Pull-Apart Bread

Lunch: Salt and Pepper Pork Belly

Dinner: Steak Fajitas

Dessert: Slime-Filled Cookies

Day 20

Breakfast: Strawberry Rhubarb Crumbles

Lunch: Hot Wings

Dinner: Black Bean Burger

Dessert: Brownie Cheesecake

Day 21

Breakfast: French Toast Sticks

Lunch: Shrimp Fajitas

Dinner: Philly Cheesesteak

Dessert: Avocado Brownies

Day 22

Breakfast: Bacon and Egg Bites

Lunch: Asian Tofu Salad

Dinner: Garlic Shrimp

Dessert: Cardamom Crinkles

Day 23

Breakfast: Spiced Applesauce Bread

Lunch: Herb Rubbed Chicken Thighs

Dinner: Chicken Bombers

Dessert: Pistachio Cookies

Day 24

Breakfast: Egg in a Hole

Lunch: Breaded Fried Shrimp

Dinner: Nana's Macaroni

Dessert: Baked Apple

Day 25

Breakfast: Breakfast Muffins

Lunch: Cauliflower Grilled Cheese

Dinner: Orange Chicken

Dessert: Pumpkin Cake

Day 26

Breakfast: Sweet Potato Toast

Lunch: Rotisserie Chicken

Dinner: Veggie Fries Medley

Dessert: Fried Banana Smores

Day 27

Breakfast: Cranberry Muffins

Lunch: Italian Breaded Eggplant

Dinner: Orange Soda Chicken Wings

Dessert: Apple Cider Snickerdoodles

Day 28

Breakfast: Bread Rolls

Lunch: Cauliflower Pizza Crust

Dinner: Crumbed Fish

Dessert: Slime-Filled Cookies

Day 29

Breakfast: Cheese and Vegetables Egg Cups

Lunch: French Fries

Dinner: Pepperoni Pita Pizza

Dessert: Brownie Cheesecake

Day 30

Breakfast: Jalapeno Cornbread

Lunch: Stuffed Mushrooms

Dinner: Breaded Whole Chicken

Dessert: Avocado Brownies

Conclusion

As you can tell by now, you can cook almost anything with your GoWise Air Fryer Oven. With the GoWise Electric Air Fryer Oven with Rotisserie and Dehydrator, you can not only fry your food but also use it for many other reasons to make a grand feast. Where traditional air fryers were only good for frying

this innovative appliance eliminates the need for extra devices. Make as many crispy dishes with low oil consumption. With the rotisserie option, roasts kebabs and entire chickens for the family. The dehydrator function allows you to make healthy fruit snacks that can last longer. You can make various spices and different types of jerky with this function. The air fryers of old were limited in capacity and versatility; now with GoWise, this is not an issue anymore.

You can then mix and match those favorites for the next 30 days and beyond. Are you excited yet? Let's get cooking!